The Gift of
The Holy Spirit

By

J. E. STILES

Price $1.50

Order from

J. E. STILES

P. O. Box 3147, Burbank, California

DEDICATION

This little book is dedicated to that great group of hungry Christians who have tarried and wept before God, longing to be filled with the Holy Spirit, whose hopes have not yet been realized. We earnestly pray that each hungry saint who reads this book shall be enabled, by its message, to rise in faith, and receive Him, for whom his heart has longed. We pray that its message of grace shall cause them to turn away from all hopes of holiness through good works, and trust only in Him, who is our righteousness. May we ever keep before us the thought of glorifying Him, who loved us and gave Himself for us, by becoming like Him, for that is the only correct objective for the Christian life.

CONTENTS

CHAPTER   PAGE

I. Have You Received the Holy Spirit Since You Believed?   7

II. Holiness   14

III. The Body of the Holy Spirit   20

IV. Misplaced Emphasis and an Incorrect Expression   23

V. Why Speak With Tongues?   30

VI. Evidences Expected in Connection with Receiving
the Holy Spirit   42

VII. Fears That Hinder   54

VIII. Receiving the Holy Spirit in the Early Church   65

IX. Reasons Why the Holy Spirit Could Not Be Given on
Basis of Our Personal Holiness   74

X. Tragedies Resulting from the Teaching That the
Holy Spirit Is Given on the Basis of Our Personal
Holiness and Consecration   81

XI. Dealing with Those Who Wish to Receive the Holy
Spirit   94

XII. Instructions to Candidates for the Holy Spirit   108

XIII. Questions and Answers   122

XIV. Some Letters Received by the Author   140

Printed in U.S.A. by
The Church Press
FARSON & SONS
GLENDALE, CALIFORNIA

At this point we print a letter that we received from a young lady who is a manager of a Bible Book Store in one of our great cities:

January 21, 1948

Dear Brother Stiles:

Praise the Lord for the Gift of the Holy Spirit. Ever since the night of November 17th when I received the Holy Spirit, my life has been changed from one of struggle to joy and peace and trust in the Lord. I feel that it is the starting point for real victorious living. I found that the Holy Spirit gives a boldness to testify and causes a real hunger for the Word. My spiritual vision has been much keener as I read and study the Bible.

Brother Stiles, I am so grateful for your teaching on "How to receive the Holy Spirit," presented in such a simple, clear way, and scripturally correct in every detail. You will never know what this has meant to me. After hearing you the first night, there rose up within me a new hope; faith began to rise—there was a chance for me after all! I had tarried so long but failed to receive. About a month before you came to the Church by the Side of the Road, I made a decision to "hold fast that which I have" and live a Christian life the best I knew *without* the Holy Spirit. I had become discouraged and down-hearted and felt inferior to those about me who had received this experience.

For several years I tarried for the Baptism of the Holy Spirit, but about three years ago I definitely decided that I must have the Holy Spirit, and tarried seriously and earnestly. The first year the Lord blessed me wonderfully and I felt the Spirit many times but the close of the revival meetings brought only disappointment. I was not discouraged, however, as I felt surely during the next year I would receive.

The second year ended with a real discouragement, and last summer during our special meetings I tarried again with a desperate determination, realizing that it would have to be now or never. It became increasingly difficult to tarry and submit to the accepted ritual—my timid nature rebelled at all this again. The Spirit did move occasionally but it was harder to pray and praise. I blindly tarried on until I was spiritually discouraged and physically exhausted and still the experience did not come.

4

What was my trouble? How I prayed that it might be revealed! Many suggestions were made to help seekers get over the "hurdle." Perhaps there was not hunger enough; or restitution needed to be made for some sin long forgotten; not good enough yet. My own thoughts were that I was not good enough and I tried sincerely, daily, to live a perfect life so that I could feel justified to *ask* God to *give* me the Holy Spirit. I searched my life thoroughly to find something that was hindering my receiving, but I could not get any satisfaction, and finally gave up tarrying. Instead of being helped, I felt torn down spiritually and physically and it finally ended in a cloud of despair settling over my life. The meeting ended; discouraged, I began to pick up the fragments of my spiritual life. I could not go on in such an unsettled state and knew that I had to make some sort of decision.

This was my state, along with many others, when God sent you along to minister to us—thank the Lord! Oh, I am so grateful for your teaching that brought light and faith to receive, not only an "experience," but a *reality* in the Gift of the Holy Spirit which enables one to live a richer and more effective Christian life and bring Glory to the Name of our Lord Jesus Christ— Praise His Name!

Sincerely and gratefully,
Irene Graham (signed).

We trust that this letter shall cause faith to rise in the hearts of many who have fallen into a similar state of discouragement, and that they shall come out into a place of rest and victory which this sister now enjoys. We print this letter because it so accurately describes the experience of multitudes of godly people, who have sought earnestly to receive the Holy Spirit, and have failed thus far to do so. The truths which caused the writer of this letter to come into her present happy state are all included in the pages of this book. May each reader believe unto righteousness, walking and talking daily with the blessed Holy Spirit.

Up to the present we have received many letters telling how this book has brought freedom, and confidence, and assurance to those who have read it. Many have struggled for years to receive the blessed Holy Spirit and their struggles have ended in complete discouragement. After reading only part of this book, in many cases, they have looked up in simple faith and received Him for whom their hearts have cried so long. Others have said they were full of doubts, fears, and questionings, but that this book has cleared away all of these.

Now, some of these letters have been very useful in bringing faith to others, helping them to step out and take from God that which is their rightful portion in Christ. If this book does for you what it has done for many others we would be most happy to have a letter from you, telling in detail what the results of reading it have been. Your letter may be just what some longing heart needs to inspire faith to receive the Holy Spirit, or to clear away misunderstandings which have kept them in doubt and uncertainty. We probably will not be able to answer your letters, but we will use them in any way possible for the glory of God. Send all letters to J. E. Stiles, P.O. Box No. 3147, Burbank, Calif.

Chapter I

HAVE YOU RECEIVED THE HOLY SPIRIT
Since you believed?

Although it is not the purpose of this little book to show that Christians of today should receive the Holy Spirit, accompanied by the supernatural evidences which we read about in the Bible account of the early church; still we feel that it would be well to include a short chapter on this subject. Many believe that all Christians receive the Holy Spirit in His fullness at the time they are saved, but this evidently is not true. We do, however, recognize the fact that no one could be saved without the work of the Holy Spirit. Jesus made a difference between the Spirit being WITH people and IN them (John 14:16-17), and surely we would not teach that any Christian is completely without the Holy Spirit. Nevertheless, we do see that there is an act of receiving the Holy Spirit after we are saved, and this receiving of Him is to give us power for Christian service. We would not be dogmatic about the exact relation entered into by this act of faith (Gal. 3:2 and 14), but it is evidently a more full and intimate relationship with the Spirit than the believer has enjoyed before taking this further step. The record in the eighth chapter of Acts certainly makes this quite clear. We quote verses 14 to 19: "Now when the apostles which were at Jerusalem heard that Samaria had received the word of God, they sent unto them Peter and John: Who, when they were come down, prayed for them, that they might receive the Holy Ghost: (For as yet he was fallen upon none of them: only they were baptized in the name of the Lord Jesus.) Then laid they their hands on them, and they received the Holy Ghost. And when Simon saw that through laying on of the apostles' hands the Holy Ghost was given, he offered them money, Saying, Give me also this power, that on whomsoever I lay hands, he may receive the Holy Ghost." Here we find that these people of Samaria had been saved, and baptized

7

in water by Philip, the evangelist, and still not one of them had received the Holy Spirit. Then it tells us that Peter and John laid hands on them and they received Him.

Now it is evident that Philip would never have knowingly baptized an unsaved man, as he was only willing to baptize the Ethiopian eunuch when he had confessed his faith in Jesus Christ as the Son of God (verses 36-38). Here we have clear evidence that these saved and baptized people still needed to receive the Holy Spirit. The first six verses of Acts 19 also show that people may or may not receive the Holy Spirit at the time they become believers. Paul said to these men at Ephesus, "Have ye received the Holy Ghost since ye believed?" This shows that the apostle Paul recognized that believers should receive the Holy Spirit after they had accepted Christ as their Saviour.

Look at Peter's statement in Acts 2:38-39, "Then Peter said unto them, Repent, and be baptized every one of you in the name of Jesus Christ for the remission of sins, and ye shall receive the gift of the Holy Ghost. For the promise is unto you, and to your children, and to all that are afar off, even as many as the Lord our God shall call." Here we find three steps which we should take to enter into the plan God has for us.

First, the sinner is to repent; then be baptized, signifying that he is burying by faith the old sinful man with evil deeds, and by faith rising up to walk in newness of life. The next step, according to Peter's statement is to receive the Holy Spirit. Certainly none would contend that Peter was suggesting that unsaved men should be baptized. But here he says that they should receive the Holy Spirit after being baptized, and therefore after being saved. If Satan cannot stop us from accepting Christ, then he will do all he can to hinder us from taking the next step toward a life of power and usefulness. Let us avail ourselves of everything God has provided to help us on in this spiritual warfare.

Of course, there are some who say that the Book of Acts recounts the events of a transition period, and that we cannot take it as applying to our situation today. Now it is quite apparent to the logical and clear thinker that the dispensation in which we live began when the Holy Spirit was given on the day of Pentecost, and will continue until the rapture of the church, when His work, preparing a bride for Christ, is completed. These people who say we cannot take the book of Acts as our pattern do so to fortify themselves in certain positions which they have taken, positions which would be completely untenable, if they accepted the Acts as applying to our present situation. Why not be fair with the Word and take it as it reads?

In addition to the fact that the book of Acts shows that Christians received the Holy Spirit after they became believers, we have Jesus' command to His disciples to receive Him. (Acts 1:4-5). Then in Matthew 28:19-20 we find Jesus saying to them, "Go ye therefore and teach all nations. . . . Teaching them to observe all things whatsoever I have commanded you . . ." He had commanded them to receive the Holy Spirit and now He tells them to teach others to do likewise. Notice how these two passages clearly make every one of us responsible to receive the Holy Spirit, if we obey the direct commands of our Saviour. Again the apostle Paul says, "Be not drunk with wine, wherein is excess; but be filled with the Spirit." (Eph. 5:18). Surely the commands of Jesus and the apostle Paul should be enough to make us realize our responsibility to receive the Holy Spirit, but there are still more reasons why we should receive Him.

We should receive Him because of what He will do in our lives to shape them into the likeness of Christ, and to make us victorious Christians, who honor the Saviour in all we do. First let us consider Acts 1:8 which reads as follows: "But ye shall receive power, after that the Holy Ghost has come upon you: and ye shall be witnesses unto me both in Jerusalem, and in all Judæa, and in Samaria, and unto the uttermost part of the earth." Here we have Jesus' statement that we shall have power to be effective witnesses after the Holy Spirit has come upon us. Now, since this is true, let us see what constitutes effective witnessing. Surely it is much more than just being a good talker. Regardless of how gifted we are as speakers, and how greatly we can sway people with our words, still we do very little that is of lasting character, if we fail to live holy lives to back up our clever words. Without doubt it is the work of the Holy Spirit to cause Christ to be formed in us (Gal. 4:19), for if He does not do it, it is certain that it never will be done. If you want to be the most effective servant of Christ then you must receive the Holy Spirit, for He alone can make you what God wants you to be.

Jesus said, "And I will pray the Father, and He shall give you another Comforter, that He may abide with you forever. Even the Spirit of truth; whom the world cannot receive, because it seeth Him not, neither knoweth Him: but ye know Him; for He dwelleth with you, and shall be in you." (John 14:16-17.) What a blessed assurance it is to the believer to know that on the Day of Pentecost this promise was fulfilled, and that the Comforter is here now, and anxious to come in and possess the life of any, who will receive Him by faith. What a heavenly privilege to have the God-given sign of speaking with other tongues as a constant reminder of His presence.

There are many who say they are in harmony with the idea of receiving the Holy Spirit, but that they are not interested in having the evidence of speaking with other tongues. We have never yet seen, or read after, any of these people who build their opposition to speaking with other tongues on the pure Word of God. They either twist the Scripture, or oppose the speaking with tongues because of what some people have done who speak with tongues. We are fully aware that many foolish, and even ungodly things have been done by those who speak with tongues, but that does not in any way change the Word of God. These people who oppose the speaking with tongues on the basis of what people have done are doing the very thing for which they themselves condemn others. When sinners reject Christ on the grounds that there are many professing Christians, who do not live as they should, these people tell them they must not go by the acts of people, but that they must take what God's Word says about salvation, accepting it as the only final authority. Why not be logical and honest, and apply the same principles everywhere?

Let us look a little farther for more benefits which will be derived from receiving the Holy Spirit. There are some very important things revealed in Jesus' words contained in John 16:13-15, "Howbeit when He, the Spirit of truth, is come, He will guide you into all truth: for He shall not speak of Himself; but whatsoever He shall hear, that shall He speak: and He will show you things to come. He shall glorify me: for He shall receive of mine, and shall show it unto you. All things that the Father hath are mine: therefore said I, that He shall take of mine, and shall show it unto you." Here Jesus reminds us that the Spirit will guide us into all truth. Do you need to be guided into all truth? Do you realize that it is the truth which sets people free? This guidance may come by making the Word of God more clear to our hearts, or by the still small voice which He speaks to those who recognize His presence, and trust Him for guidance. Notice again, Jesus says, "He shall glorify me." Is it not of utmost importance that Jesus shall be glorified in our eyes? For it is as we get an enlarged vision of Him, that we shall become more like Him. Not only will the Spirit reveal Christ to those who receive Him, but by His working in them He will cause them to be formed into the likeness of the Saviour, and thus He will be revealed to others. Do you want others to see Christ in you? If so, then receive the Holy Spirit, and let Him start the work of transforming you into the likeness of our blessed Lord. Others will never see Jesus in you until you become like Him. Oh! the heavenly privilege of having Him abiding in these bodies of ours, to guide and instruct and reveal Christ to us, and then in turn through us revealing Christ to others. I John 3:2 tells us that we shall one day be like Jesus for we shall see Him as He is. Our vision of Christ here and now is only partial at best, but to the extent that we really see Him, we become like Him, and since the Spirit will reveal Him to us, as He abides within, surely we should joyfully receive Him, if we have a heart purpose to be like Jesus.

Turning to the eighth chapter of Romans we find a number of most interesting statements. Verse 11 tells us that the Spirit will quicken our mortal bodies if He dwells in us. Now there is in this statement a reference to the coming resurrection, but we believe it also has a present application; the idea being that the Spirit will renew our physical vigor, as we recognize His presence, and trust Him to do so.

Verse 13 tells us that it is by the Spirit that we mortify the deeds of the body, or cause to die those carnal desires which are detrimental to our spiritual life and development. "Walk in the Spirit, and ye shall not fulfill the lusts of the flesh," is the statement of Galatians 5:16. Do you need to subdue your natural evil tendencies? If so reach out by faith and receive the Holy Spirit, that you, by His power, may live a life of victory.

What Christian has not felt the need of help to pray more effectively? In verses 26 and 27 we have the assurance that the Spirit will help us in prayer, because we do not know how to pray as we ought, but He, knowing all things, and being all powerful, will supply our lack, and lead us into a prayer life of real power.

We might consider briefly at this point the attitude of those who interpret I Cor. 13:8-12 to mean that all these supernatural signs were to cease when the Bible was complete. The passage reads as follows: "Charity never faileth: but whether there be prophecies, they shall fail; whether there be tongues, they shall cease; whether there be knowledge, it shall vanish away. For we know in part, and we prophesy in part. But when that which is perfect is come, then that which is in part shall be done away. When I was a child, I spake as a child, I understood as a child, I thought as a child: but when I became a man, I put away childish things. For now we see through a glass, darkly; but then face to face: now I know in part; but then shall I know even as also I am known." These people say that the Bible is "that which is perfect," and that since we have it in its complete form, we no longer have need of these super-natural gifts of the Spirit. We admit that the Bible is perfect, but our understanding of it is imperfect; therefore, we still see through a glass darkly. They say tongues have ceased, but they say nothing about knowledge vanishing away, and these statements are in the same sentence. This passage also says that "when that which is perfect is come" we shall see face to face, and not through a glass darkly. Since it is evident that we still see as through a glass darkly, then it is also evident that "that which is perfect" is not yet come. We feel that this statement can refer only to the return of our Lord, and when He comes, everything that is in part shall be done away, because it shall be swallowed up in the glorious revelation of the whole, which is in Him. These sign gifts will continue until He comes and we are made perfectly into His likeness and have all knowledge and understanding.

Some also say that those who had a separate experience of receiving the Holy Spirit, as recorded in the Book of Acts, needed it to make them fully New Testament Christians. They claim that these people had had some kind of an Old Testament experience, including repentance, as preached by John the Baptist, and needed to receive the Holy Spirit to bring their experience up to New Testament standards. This is evidently not true, as all the people who are said to have received the Holy Spirit after Pentecost were definitely saved after Pentecost. In the case of the Samaritans (Acts 8) it is evident that they were saved as a result of Philip's preaching. Saul was saved on the Damascus road (Acts 9:1-17). The people at the house of Cornelius were evidently not saved before Peter went there, as we are told (Acts 11:14) that the angel said to Cornelius that Peter would tell him words by which he and all his house should be saved. (See Acts 10:34-48.) The men at Ephesus were not saved when Paul went there because they had only heard the message of John the Baptist preached to them by Apollos. (See Acts 19:1-7; 18:24-26.) Now it is altogether a mistaken idea to suppose that these various groups were not really saved people, as those who receive Christ today are saved. They needed to receive the Holy Spirit after they were saved, and we also have the same need.

With all these evidences that we should receive the Holy Spirit, and all the assurances of blessing to those who will receive Him, it would seem to us a strange thing that any Christian would neglect this glorious opportunity which God has given to all His children. It should thrill our hearts to their very depths to realize that we may have the same Holy Spirit abiding in us, who was in the apostles of old. Let us reach out by faith and receive Him at once.

Chapter II

HOLINESS!

Luke 6:45: ". . . for of the abundance of the heart his mouth speaketh."

Lest someone might think that we do not teach and preach holiness of life and character, because we say that any Christian, in his present state of development is ready to, and can, receive the Holy Spirit at once, therefore we feel that we should go into this matter of holiness and Christian character right at the beginning of this little book on the subject of the Holy Spirit.

Let us say without further ado that there is no other correct final objective for the Christian life than to be fully like Jesus. Many people have said to the writer that they would be satisfied if they barely made Heaven in the end, as those described in I Corinthians 3:11-15; and our answer has been that they should be ashamed to have such a low objective. Certainly there is something far more important than just to get eternal life, and that is that we should fully honor Him who loved us and gave Himself for us. And how may we fully honor Him? Our answer is, by being like Him.

We believe that God has provided in Christ everything that is needed for our lives to be shaped into His likeness, and to that end we have written the contents of this book. Shall we examine and see just what righteousness and true holiness really is?

Many people have thought that holiness consisted in conforming to a certain set of standards which they set up, and this is not true at all. A person may conform to all the standards of conduct that you set up before him, and still have a heart full of sin, even though these standards which he measures up to are entirely right and good. A man may not steal because he is afraid of public opinion, or of getting caught by the officers, and still be a thief at heart. He may not commit adultery for the same, or other reasons, and still be an adulterer in God's sight. Jesus said, "Whosoever looketh on a woman to lust after her hath committed adultery with her already in his heart." (Matt. 5:28).

Holiness is a matter of the heart entirely. It never was and never will be brought about by good deeds or right conduct. Good works and right conduct are the inevitable results of a holy heart, but never the cause of holiness, since holy hearts are produced by God alone. He only can change us, and put a clean heart within us. Righteousness is by faith, and not by works of any kind. In Rom. 10:1-4 we read, "Brethren, my heart's desire and prayer to God for Israel is, that they might be saved. For I bear them record that they have a zeal of God, but not according to knowledge. For they being ignorant of God's righteousness, and going about to establish their own righteousness, have not submitted themselves unto the righteousness of God. For Christ is the end of the law for righteousness to every one that believeth." A great many people carefully measure up to certain standards which they set up, and still they are so full of pride and self righteousness that they are obnoxious to God. Not only are they full of pride, but they are completely merciless with others who do not measure up to their set of rules, or fit into their mold. We must realize that sin is deliberately doing that which we know to be wrong in God's sight, and others may do things which you cannot do, and still be walking in the way of holiness. It is all a matter of the light people have on these various things.

A great American preacher was in a Christian home in a foreign country, and the lady of the house set a glass of wine on the table at each meal. This same lady said to the visiting minister, "Brother, is it possible that Christians drink coffee in America?" Now to her coffee drinking was entirely wrong for Christians, and still she saw nothing wrong at all with drinking a glass of wine at the meals. She would be just as horrified at a Christian getting drunk as you or I would be, but she saw nothing wrong with a single glass of wine. She could drink a glass of wine without feeling condemnation, but we could not, because we know the first glass of spiritous liquor has started many on the way to being drunkards. We only use this illustration to show that we cannot judge what is in the other man's heart, even though he does things which we could not do.

Some will say that sin is sin wherever you find it, and to them sinning means that you do the things which they think to be wrong. The other man has just as much right to say that you are sinning because you do things which he thinks to be wrong. If we are logical in our thinking we will have to come back to the fact that holiness and sinfulness are states of heart, and the things we do simply indicate our condition of heart. Can a man whose heart is full of the love of Jesus deliberately go out and follow sinful practices? No indeed! If he loves the Lord he will naturally want to do those things which are pleasing to Him. We do not have to worry about the conduct of the man who really loves the Lord. On the other hand, it does no good to be cutting and lashing at people because of the things they do, which we feel to be wrong. In doing that we are only dealing with symptoms, and not with the real disease. Get the man's heart right and his conduct will begin to change and get right.

Now God never gave the Holy Spirit as a reward because the Christian had gone a long way in building Christian character. He gave the Holy Spirit to come in and do in the Christian that which he cannot do in, and for himself. We have clearly shown elsewhere that it is illogical and unscriptural to tell a Christian that he has to do this or that in order to be worthy to receive the Holy Spirit. The only thing that makes any of us worthy to receive anything from God is the imputed righteousness of Christ which is credited to the account of those who will believe. Romans 10:10 says, "For with the heart man believeth unto righteousness." No man is worthy to receive the Holy Spirit, or ever will be, in his own righteousness, but he must come clothed in the righteousness of Christ which is by FAITH. The people who tell seekers that they must clean up and get more righteous before they can receive the Holy Spirit are defeating the very thing they are trying to promote. They are trying to get the man formed into the likeness of Christ, and it is only the Holy Spirit who can do this. The Holy Spirit does not come into us because we have gone a long way in the building of Christian character, but He comes in to form that character in us which will make us Christlike. By telling a Christian that he must get more victorious and holy before he can receive the Holy Spirit, we shut him off from the very source of holiness, and victorious living.

Our standing before God is entirely the result of faith in what Christ has done for us, and it is only in Him that we have any standing at all before the throne of God, "Therefore being justified by faith, we have peace with God through our Lord Jesus Christ." (Rom. 5:1.) "For as many as are of the works of the law are under the curse: for it is written, Cursed is every one that continueth not in all things which are written in the book of the law to do them. But that no man is justified by the law in the sight of God, it is evident: for, The just shall live by faith." (Gal. 3:10-11.) Since it is His righteousness, which is by faith, that gives me a standing before God, therefore we have a standing which is as perfect as the standing which Christ has in the presence of the Father. And how perfect is that? Absolutely and completely perfect. "Ye are complete in Him." (Col. 2:10.) Let us never forget that a Christian has an absolutely perfect standing before God, since we are "complete in Him," "Accepted in the Beloved," or else he has no standing at all, and is a lost soul, clear outside the fold. Such a thing as a person having a good, or fair, or poor standing before God is entirely unscriptural, without the slightest foundation in God's Word. We are either saved or unsaved, and as such, we either have a perfect standing in God's family, or no standing at all.

A great many people have never come to understand the difference between our standing, and our state, and thus have been greatly confused. Jesus used the expression, "Ye must be born again" to show that the relation between Christ and the saved one is like the relation between parent and child. The moment a child is born his standing in the family is established, and does not change. He is as perfectly a member of the family as he ever can be. He is perfect in his standing in the family. His legal claims on his parents are as complete as they ever will be. His right of inheritance is by birth and not because of his age or development. Now the state of development of that child is something entirely different from his standing. His state is changing every day, going forward toward full manhood or womanhood, but all during this development his standing, or position in the family, never changes a particle. Now the same thing is true in God's family. Our standing is perfect, because we stand in Christ's righteousness, but our state of development is changing every day. We are either going forward to be more like Christ, or we are going backward and becoming less like Him. Sad to say, God has many children who have never gone very far forward in developing into the likeness of Christ. If they could only realize that they can do nothing by struggling against their natural evil tendencies, to make themselves more holy or good, then they might throw themselves unreservedly upon the Lord, and trust Him to do in them, and for them, by His Spirit, that which they never could do in and for themselves. The universal testimony of all great Christians of the past or present is that the fullness of blessing and spiritual development comes only to those who will make a complete consecration to God, putting themselves entirely in His hands, and then trusting Him recklessly, to receive what they have committed to Him, and to shape them into the likeness of Christ. Oh! that we might learn to trust Him for righteousness instead of trying to produce it by the efforts of the natural man. All our efforts will produce are the works of the flesh. (See Gal. 5:19-21.)

Let us illustrate this point. Here is a woman who is as faithful and regular as a clock in seeing that the church is beautifully decorated with flowers every Sunday. She makes a lot of sacrifice, and goes to considerable expense to do this service. Now it looks outwardly as if this woman is really doing a lot for God, but just let someone else re-arrange one of her vases of flowers, and she is highly insulted at once. "Here I do all this work week after week, and give my time and money to beautify the church, and then they are not satisfied with the way I do it. If they don't like my work they can just do it themselves, as far as I am concerned. I'm done. I've slaved, and sacrificed and this is all the thanks I get for it, etc., etc." Was that woman doing that work for the love of Christ, or was she doing it to get the praise of men? We leave the reader to judge that question. What she did was a right and good thing to do, but the motive behind the doing of it was entirely wrong. Her heart was full of malice and pride right in the midst of work which was supposed to be for the Lord.

Yes, dear reader, holiness is a matter of the heart and not that which appears on the surface. Let us determine that we will put ourselves completely at God's disposal, and then trust Him to produce holy hearts within us, by the power of His Spirit. If we do that we need have no fear that our acts will be wrong or our behavior displeasing to Him.

Chapter III

THE BODY OF THE HOLY SPIRIT

A great many Christians seem to think that they are free to use their bodies in any way they please, and that they will have to answer for their doings to no one. There is a very solemnizing thought in the first verse of Romans the twelfth chapter, which reads, "I beseech you therefore, brethren, by the mercies of God, that ye present your bodies a living sacrifice, holy, acceptable unto God, which is your reasonable service." We are told here to present our bodies a living sacrifice to God, but there is no mention as to which one of the Blessed Trinity it is, to whom these bodies of ours are to be presented.

Since we are here in this world it must be that we are to present our bodies to the member of the Godhead who is here, and that, of course, is the Holy Spirit. The Holy Spirit came into this world without a body, seeking bodies through which He could do the work of God in the world, and as we yield our bodies to Him, they become, in reality His body. He has no body through which to work, except your body and mine. Our ears are His ears to hear the cry of the distressed, and our feet His feet to run on errands of mercy for Him. He has no eyes but ours to see the misery and sorrow of those about us, and our hands must minister as His hands to the sin-sick world.

In I Cor. :19-20 we read, "What? know ye not that your body is the temple of the Holy Ghost which is in you, which ye have of God, and ye are not your own? For ye are bought with a price: therefore glorify God in your body, and in your spirit, which are God's." Here we have the statement that our bodies are temples of the Holy Spirit, and in a kind of a way we have believed this, but to most of us it has never become a living reality that our bodies actually become the body of the Holy Spirit, when we receive Him by faith. Here we are taught that we are not our own, but are bought with a price, and if we will

20

stop and think, we will realize that the price was tremendous which was paid for us. Only the life of God's Son was sufficient to meet the demands of the law, and pay the penalty which should have fallen on you and me. When we think of the crucified Son of God suffering the tortures of the damned in our behalf, it makes us realize the value God places on us.

See also Eph. 1:18, "The eyes of your understanding being enlightened: that ye may know what is the hope of His calling, and what the riches of the glory of His inheritance in the saints." Here it is pointed out that God has a great inheritance in the saints, and if we fail to use these lives and these bodies for His glory, we are cheating Him out of the inheritance which is rightfully His. Notice, it says in this passage which we quoted in I Cor. 6.19-20, "Therefore glorify God in your body." Since this body of ours actually becomes the body of the Holy Spirit, then there is resting on us a tremendous responsibility to use it in a way that is fitting for the Holy Spirit's body to be used. "Ye are not your own, for ye are bought with a price."

We all feel that the Virgin Mary was greatly honored in that she was selected by God to be the one woman in all the world through whom He would prepare a body for His Son. The angel said, "Hail, thou that art highly favored, the Lord is with thee: blessed art thou among women." (Luke 1:28). Some groups go so far as to worship Mary, because of her selection by the Lord for this great honor. God provided a body for His Son, the second person of the blessed Trinity, through one woman, but the thought may never have come to you that He has extended to every born again saint just as great an honor as He extended to that one woman, in that we have the exalted privilege of providing a body for the third person of the Trinity, who is very God just as truly as was Jesus. What a stupendous truth is here. Can you carelessly use this body of yours when you realize that it is also His body?

Every act that these bodies of ours perform should be an act worthy of the blessed Holy Spirit. In so far as we yield ourselves, body, soul and spirit to the Holy Spirit, to that extent our acts are His acts, and our thoughts are His thoughts. On the other hand, to the extent that we fail to yield ourselves to Him our acts are the works of the flesh, and not glorifying to God. Remember, this life and this body of yours is a sacred trust that has been given to you. You are a steward who will give an account some day to our blessed Master for the way you have administered the estate which has been entrusted to you.

Let us never forget, as Spirit-filled saints, that our bodies are His body, and therefore we should glorify God in our bodies and in our spirits which are God's.

Chapter IV

MISPLACED EMPHASIS
and
AN INCORRECT EXPRESSION

For nearly half of the twenty-odd years since we received the blessed Holy Spirit, and became connected with this Full Gospel movement, which has circled the globe, we have seen very clearly that entirely too much emphasis has been laid on the initial experience of receiving the Holy Spirit, as compared to the emphasis laid on the subsequent walk in the Spirit, which should follow His coming in to abide. Now we do not mean to intimate that we should cease to lay great stress upon the receiving of the Spirit. That is of fundamental importance. What we do wish to emphasize is the importance of the walk in the Holy Spirit which should follow on to the end of our earthly career. No experience of today will supply the need of tomorrow, regardless of how wonderful it may be. The Israelites of old found that manna kept over for the next day bred worms and stunk. Yes, it had to be gathered fresh every day, and surely this applies to the spiritual manna upon which we feed our souls.

We have strongly urged the candidate, who comes to receive the Holy Spirit, to make a complete consecration of all that he has and is, telling him that obedience to the leading of the Spirit is fundamental in getting ourselves ready to receive Him. We certainly would not discount consecration and obedience to God. Every Christian, whether he is seeking the Holy Spirit or not, should realize that the responsibility to obey, and make a full consecration to the Lord, rests upon him. No one ever had the fullness of God's blessing and approval, nor did he ever develop the Christian character God wants to see in him, until he has come to that place of full surrender, where all is put into the hands of our loving Father.

The point, however, which we want to emphasize is that the

great test of consecration and obedience is going to come after we have received the Holy Spirit. Multitudes have received Him, and then afterwards they have not been willing to walk in the way He would lead them. That is why the Apostle Paul had to write as he did to the Corinthians, telling them that they were yet carnal, and babes in Christ. If people are taught that the receiving of the Holy Spirit is just learning the first simple lesson in co-operating with His movings in their lives, and that their subsequent walk in the Spirit is the thing of primary importance, then there is less tendency to feel self satisfied, considering that they have arrived at a desired end. So far as we can see, it will not do you much good to receive the Holy Spirit if you are not prepared to follow on through the years as He would guide and instruct you. On the other hand, let us remember that He will give us strength and courage to follow on if we are willing to put ourselves completely in His hands.

The initial experience of receiving the Holy Spirit is only important in that it constitutes the beginning of a fellowship which should be constant and permanent. So often it has been made very apparent, by the testimonies of Spirit-filled people, that they believed that the Holy Spirit was in them only when they felt some special moving, when in reality He was there all the time. If you will listen to the testimonies of Spirit-filled people, especially at some of our great annual camp meetings, you will hear a considerable number that run something like this: "I came to camp meeting last year feeling very much down in spirits, but the third night I was here the power of God came down in a wonderful way, and I got gloriously refilled. I spoke with other tongues for an hour and a half, and it was such a wonderful refreshing. I really lived in another world for a solid week. It seemed as if I hardly touched the ground, I was so lost in God and heavenly things. About that time we had to go home, and I began the daily round of duties that kept me busy from morning till night. Well, it just seemed that I was so busy with cooking, and washing and sewing, and added to that, the tying up of cut fingers, and kissing of bumped heads, that I didn't have much time to read my Bible, or pray as I should. Little by little the joy seemed to slip away, and it wasn't long until I felt as if I was in a spiritual desert. I was so dried up and so hungry. How I have been looking forward for months to this year's camp meeting so that I could be filled again. Well, last night it came, and Oh! how the glory poured down on me. I surely feel like a new person today. I spoke in other tongues for hours, and words can't express how wonderful it was. Heaven really came down and flooded my heart to overflowing. Praise the Lord for His wonderful goodness to me." Now some people might feel that such a testimony was splendid and beautiful, but we feel that it is a tragedy for any one to have to give a testimony like that. If it were plotted on cross section paper the curve would look much like a temperature chart in the weather bureau office. Her Christian life is made up of a few precious experiences spaced far apart, and the rest of the time her spiritual weather chart shows from cool to sub-zero temperatures. Now having these blessed experiences occasionally is far better than not having them at all, but if those who give such testimonies would get a correct understanding of God's plan for them, and realize that the Holy Spirit is, in reality, a Person who has come to abide constantly, they might have had blessed fellowship with Him all the time, which would have kept them steadily going on to higher heights spiritually. We wonder, when we hear such a testimony, if the person giving it will sag down to a low level again, and need to be refreshed at next camp meeting. Probably most of these people, giving such testimonies, will not speak with other tongues again until next camp meeting, or some other special meeting during the year, when God's plan is that they would worship Him every day, using this supernatural means of spiritual up-building.

We are not discouraging in any sense special meetings, and camps for the purpose of spiritual revival and refreshing. We all need it at times, but we do say that there is no reason to sag down into the same old rut after the refreshing experience. We should thank God for it, and go on in real faith to climb up to greater victories than we have ever known. Will we ever learn that real spirituality is not measured by our feelings? Let us go on trusting God on the basis of what His Word says, regardless of feelings, and we will find ourselves making real spiritual progress. Let us get it firmly fixed in our minds that the Holy Spirit is come to abide forever (John 14:16), and that He is ready to guide and lead us, and respond to faith on our part, whenever we step out and exercise it.

The other point on which we wish to lay emphasis in this chapter concerns the use of a term which we feel is mis-leading, and through its use many earnest people have gotten mistaken ideas concerning the receiving of the Holy Spirit. Now in speaking about receiving the Holy Spirit, we have almost universally used the expression, "The Baptism of the Holy Spirit." We have asked people, "Have you received the Baptism?" when inquiring whether they had received the Holy Spirit or not. We would not be dogmatic on this point, or say that those expressions are wrong. We believe, however, that we would do better, in conveying to the minds of seekers for the Holy Spirit, the idea we want them to get, if we would use the terms used in the early church.

Let us stop for a moment and consider what it is we are trying to convey to the mind of the one who has not yet received the Spirit. Since the Holy Spirit is a Person, it seems to us that we should do our best to lead people to realize that they are receiving HIM into their hearts and bodies, to abide forever. (See I Cor. 6:19-20 and John 14:16-17.) The very term "baptism" suggests a single event which occurs, and is finished, and then becomes something that is in the past. Now we recognize that John the Baptist said, "I indeed baptize you with water: but One mightier than I cometh, the latchet of whose shoes I am not worthy to unloose. He shall baptize you with the Holy Ghost and with fire." (Luke 3:16; Matt. 3:11; Mark 1:8; John 1:33.) This was before Pentecost. We also realize that Jesus said, as recorded in Acts 1:5, "For John truly baptized with water; but ye shall be baptized with the Holy Ghost not many days hence." This also was prior to, and referring to the coming of the Holy Ghost upon the waiting disciples, on the Day of Pentecost.

Now the coming of the Holy Spirit on that day was a fulfillment of John's prediction (Matt. 3:11; Mark 1:8; Luke 3:16; John 1:33), and Jesus' promise as told in John 14:16-17, "And I will pray the Father, and He shall give you another Comforter, that He may abide with you forever; even the Spirit of truth; whom the world cannot receive, because it seeth Him not, neither knoweth Him: but ye know Him; for He dwelleth with you, and shall be in you." (See also John 15:26-27.) On that day the part played by the Father (John 14:16-17) and the Son (Luke 3:16) in the matter of the Holy Spirit's coming, was done and completed, just as Jesus' part in providing salvation for the world was finished, when He died on the cross, rose from the dead, and ascended into Heaven, to take His place as our advocate at the right hand of the Father. All was completed. From that day to this, man's salvation has not depended on the Father or the Son doing anything. Their part is done. The only part played by the Godhead in our salvation in this dispensation, is the convicting of of the Holy Spirit, which brings man to a realization of his sinfulness, his need of a Savior, and the perfect provision that has been already made to meet his need. After the Spirit does His part, it rests with the man entirely to accept, or reject, the salvation provided by Christ's sacrifice. It is not now a question of God's willingness to save any man. That was settled nearly two thousand years ago. The great question, the all important question is this: Will the man receive the salvation so graciously provided? (See II Cor. 5:18-20; John 1:12; Acts 16:31.)

The same thing is true concerning the receiving of the Holy Spirit that is true of our salvation. The Holy Spirit is here, acting as the representative of the Godhead in this dispensation. It is not now a question of God's willingness to fill Christians with the Spirit. That question was settled when the Spirit was given at Pentecost. It is now a matter of the dealing of man with the Holy Spirit, and the Holy Spirit with man. The present question is this: Will the man receive the Holy Spirit who is here, ready to enter any saved man's soul and body, who will open his heart's door, and let Him in? Never forget, your *body* is the temple of the Holy Spirit. Since it is Jesus that is spoken of as baptizing with the Holy Spirit, and since His part is done, we feel that the whole church was potentially baptized with the Holy Spirit on the Day of Pentecost, just as all men were potentially saved by Christ's redemptive work at Calvary. Therefore, today, all that is necessary for a man to do to avail himself of the gift of salvation, is to repent of his sin, and receive Christ as his Savior; so likewise in order to be filled with the Holy Spirit the saved man has only to receive Him by faith. (Acts 2:38-39; Gal. 3:2, 5, 14.)

We find that the expression "baptized with the Holy Ghost" is never used after Pentecost except once, (Acts 11:16) when Peter quotes what Jesus said in Acts 1:5. Therefore, let us examine the expressions used in connection with the receiving of the Holy Spirit in the early apostolic church, i. e., after Pentecost.

The first case is found in Acts, chapter 8, where we have the record of Philip's great revival at Samaria. In the 17th verse we read, "Then laid they their hands on them, and they received the Holy Ghost." It does not say, "they received the baptism" or "the baptism of the Holy Ghost." It says, "They received the Holy Ghost," which conveys the idea that they received a Person into their lives, and that is the idea we want people to get, for that is what really happens.

The next recorded instance is in Acts 9:1-17, where it recounts the story of Saul's dynamic conversion on the Damascus road, and his being led blind into the city, to sit for three days in the house of Judas. Then God spoke to a man by the name of Ananias and told him to go and minister to Saul. Now let us read verse 17, "And Ananias went his way, and entered into the house; and putting his hands on him said. Brother Saul, the Lord, even Jesus, that appeared unto thee in the way as thou camest, hath sent me, that thou mightest receive thy sight, and be filled with the Holy Ghost." Notice again, it does not speak of being baptized with the Holy Ghost, nor does it speak of being "filled with the baptism," as we have often heard it expressed. No, it says ". . . and be filled with the Holy Ghost." Again, this expression conveys the idea of a person coming into the believer to abide in him. Truly the Holy Spirit is a Person, and we never should forget it.

Let us now look in Acts 10:1-49 at the extended story of Peter going to the house of Cornelius in Caesarea. When Peter finally began to preach to the company that Cornelius had gathered we read (v. 44), "While Peter yet spake these words, the Holy Ghost fell on all them which heard the Word." Here we have a different expression, but it does not say. *"The Baptism* fell on all them that heard the Word." No, it says "The Holy Ghost fell on all." Again the expression is such as to give the idea of the coming of a person upon them. Then in verse 47 we notice that Peter did not say, "Can any man forbid water, that these should not be baptized, which have received 'the baptism of' the Holy Ghost as well as we." No, he said, "Received the Holy Ghost as well as we." Now the term "baptism of the Holy Ghost" suggests that it is something which the Holy Ghost does or gives, when in reality He, Himself, comes in to abide, as we open the door by faith to receive *Him.*

Let us now turn to Acts 19:1-6 and read Paul's meeting with the men at Ephesus. In verse 6 we read, "And when Paul had laid his hands upon them, the Holy Ghost came on them; and they spake with tongues, and prophesied." Here we find the record telling us "the Holy Ghost came on them." It does not say anything about the *baptism* coming on them, or their receiving the baptism. It again correctly expresses the idea that the Lord wants the seeker to get, namely, the idea of a Person Himself coming in to take up His abode.

Now, after considering every Scripture where it is recorded that people received the Holy Spirit in the early Apostolic Church it is very apparent that they NEVER used the term "Baptized with the Holy Ghost" or "Baptism of the Holy Ghost." These Scriptures always spoke of the Person, the Holy Ghost, coming on them or their receiving the Holy Ghost, or being filled with the Holy Ghost. Does it not appear that we would do better in helping the uninstructed if we would use the same terms and expressions which the Apostles themselves used? We leave the reader to answer this question for himself.

Chapter V

WHY SPEAK WITH TONGUES?

Jesus said, "In my name shall they cast out devils; they shall speak with new tongues; etc." (Mark 16:17.) The Apostle Paul said, "I would that ye all spake with tongues," (I Cor. 14:5,) also, "I thank my God, I speak with tongues more than ye all." (verse 18.) There has been much misunderstanding concerning this matter of speaking with other tongues, which has, in some cases, brought much damage to the cause of Christ, and, certainly, has robbed multitudes of the blessing which God intended them to have.

One thing is certain; it is not a subject to be lightly cast aside as unimportant in the church of Jesus Christ. God does not have His Book filled with things of minor importance, or unnecessary statements. Jesus did not say that a few believers shall speak with tongues. He certainly implied that all believers should do so, as does also the Apostle Paul. Why then is it that most of the believers in Jesus, in the world today, do not speak with tongues, as Jesus said they would? There are a number of reasons for this condition, but the most important seems to be that there has been very little sound, logical, and scriptural teaching as to the scope and value of this gift from God. People have not understood what actually happens when a person speaks with other tongues, nor have they realized the value derived from the exercise of this gift. It is the aim of this chapter to clear up some of the mistaken ideas which many have had, so that more may be partakers of the blessings God intended for them.

The failure to understand what actually happens when a person speaks in other tongues not only exists among those who do not, but also among those who do speak with tongues, under the anointing of the Holy Spirit. If we will carefully examine what the Bible teaches on this subject, it will be evident, to any earnest seeker for truth, that the Apostle Paul definitely encourages the practice of speaking with other tongues for a number of different reasons. From our own experiences, and from the testimony of many others, both ministers and laymen, we are convinced that every Spirit-filled child of God should speak with other tongues every day, IN HIS OWN PRIVATE PRAYER LIFE. We are therefore setting forth a number of reasons for this practice, both in our private prayer life, and otherwise.

1. "He that speaketh in an unknown tongue edifieth himself;" (I Cor. 14:4.) Of all the nine gifts of the Spirit mentioned in I Cor. 12, speaking with tongues is the only one spoken of as being edifying to the person who exercises the gift. Our mental faculties are not quickened or improved by this exercise, but our spiritual faculties are greatly built up and strengthened. It is the testimony of many Christians that spending much time praying in other tongues has been a great source of spiritual power and blessing. "For if I pray in an unknown tongue, my spirit prayeth, but my understanding is unfruitful. What is it then? I will pray with the spirit, and I will pray with the understanding also: I will sing with the spirit, and I will sing with the understanding also." From these verses in I Cor. 14:14-15 we find that Paul followed the practice of praying with other tongues, and points out that in so doing he was praying with the spirit. Notice! He does not say that the Holy Spirit prays, but he says, "*My* spirit prayeth." Of course, the Holy Spirit is miraculously guiding the speaking, but the man is doing the speaking by an act of his will. We will discuss this point further at a later time.

In verses 18 and 19 we read, "I thank my God, I speak with tongues more than ye all: yet in the church I had rather speak five words with my understanding, that by my voice I might teach others also, then ten thousand words in an unknown tongue." Here we find that he spoke with tongues a great deal in private, but he points out the foolishness of speaking with tongues in the public meeting unless, of course, there is an interpretation, so that the church might be edified and blessed. "I would that ye all spake with tongues, but rather that ye prophesied: for greater is he that prophesieth than he that speaketh with tongues, except he interpret, that the church may receive edifying." (I Cor. 14:5) "If any man speak in an unknown tongue, let it be by two, or at the most by three, and that by course; and let one interpret. But if there be no interpreter, let him keep silence in the church; and let him speak to himself, and to God." (I Cor. 14:27-28.)

2. "He that speaketh in an unknown tongue speaketh not unto men, but unto God: for no man understandeth him; howbeit in the spirit he speaketh mysteries." (Weymouth's translation says, "Divine secrets") I Cor. 14:2. If God has given us a divine, supernatural means of communion with Him, which is not of the mind, but of the spirit; surely it is not something to be lightly cast aside as being unimportant. God has nothing extra in His Word, which is not there for a purpose. What a glorious privilege to be able to whisper divine secrets to our heavenly Bridegroom in a language which He has supernaturally given us. It is outside the realm of our intellect, but our spirit understands and rejoices in this heavenly communion. It also delights me to believe that when I commune with God in this supernatural way, I have Satan shut out so that he cannot listen in. We do not say that we know this is true, but Weymouth's translation of verse 2 surely suggests it.

3. Speaking with tongues helps to keep us always conscious of the presence of the Holy Spirit within us. If by any means we can be kept constantly conscious of His presence, it will vitally affect the way we live, and cause us to be more Christlike. If Jesus could walk right by your side continuously for a week, as He walked with Peter and John, do you think it would have a decided effect upon the way you lived and conducted yourself? Well, He is really even closer than that, He is within you. An experience of the writer will help to illustrate this truth.

While conducting a week's Bible conference, on the subject of the Holy Spirit, in a certain church, we stayed with a family who lived in an apartment under the rear part of the church. One day we entered the kitchen and at once saw that something was decidedly wrong between the mother and twelve year old daughter. Figuratively speaking, the sparks were really flying. As soon as the daughter saw me come in she took hold of my coat sleeve and started leading me toward another room, saying that she wanted to talk to me. When the door closed she said, with tears in her eyes, "Brother Stiles, I want you to pray for me. I get angry sometimes and talk back to Mother when she tells me to do something which I do not want to do, and I know it is wrong." I said to her, "Let us go up in the church and talk this over." As soon as we were seated on the edge of the carpeted platform, I said, "E . . ., are you saved?" "Oh! yes, Brother Stiles, I know I am saved," she replied. "And E . . ., haven't you received the Holy Spirit?" I asked. "Yes, I have," was her immediate answer. "Now, E . . .," I said, "Suppose I had been standing right beside you when you became angry, and talked back to your mother a few minutes ago?" "Oh! Brother Stiles, I would have been ashamed to act that way if you had been there," she replied. "But E . . ., do you not realize that the thing you did was done right in the very presence of the Holy Spirit, who is in you?" I continued. She looked at me with incredulous eyes for a moment, and then dropped on her knees and began to cry as if her heart would break. How she cried to the Lord to forgive her sin! Soon she felt the assurance that she was forgiven and, with raised hands, she began praising God with other tongues. I quietly got up and slipped away, leaving her with the Lord. I never knew how long she stayed there that day, as the subject was not mentioned again while I was there.

About a month later I was in their town so I stopped to see these friends. Almost as soon as I was inside the hause, the daughter took hold of my sleeve and started leading me toward the other room. "I want to tell you something," she said, "something that will make you glad." As soon as we were in the other room and the door was shut, she looked at me, with a sly twinkle in her eye, and said, "Brother Stiles, I haven't got mad any more." You see, she had been made conscious of the fact that the Holy Spirit was right there in her all the time to see whatever she did, and it had decidedly affected her life. Now her speaking with other tongues was a powerful factor in keeping her conscious of His continued presence, and so it will be in the life of anyone who will follow the practice of praying with the spirit every day.

4. Praying with other tongues eliminates the possibility of selfishness entering into our prayers. As long as our minds decide what to pray about, there is always the possibility of selfishness entering in; but when we pray in other tongues we do not know what we are praying about, but the Holy Spirit is directing that.

Therefore, since He is deciding what we pray, the possibility of selfishness entering in is eliminated. "Likewise the Spirit also helpeth our infirmities: for we know not what we should pray for as we ought: but the Spirit itself maketh intercession for us with groanings which cannot be uttered." (Rom. 8:26.) Everyone of us will have to admit the fact that we have at times prayed selfishly. It may be we did not realize it at the time, but later we saw that our prayers were decidedly selfish, and often times prayed in self-pity. However, when we allow the Holy Spirit to decide what we pray, and it is our spirit that prays, rather than our intellect, we know that our praying is not selfish, and is in line with the will of God.

5. Praying with other tongues helps me to learn to more fully trust God. Since the Holy Spirit supernaturally directs the words I speak, faith must be exercised, as I do not know what the next word is to be. I am trusting God for that. Trusting Him in one line helps me to trust Him in other lines.

6. "For our conversation (citizenship) is in Heaven ..." (Phil. 3:20.) Heaven is my home country; I am only a pilgrim and wanderer here for a few short years. How natural it should be for me to pray with other tongues, which Paul says is praying with the Spirit, and surely it is our spiritual life which comes most directly in contact with the heavenly realm. We can live, by faith, in heavenly places right now (Eph. 2:6), and surely praying in other tongues helps us to do so.

We read in the Word that Abraham considered himself as being here only temporarily, but he constantly looked forward toward eternal things which had permanent foundations. Should not we, like Abraham, have our faces set toward home; and will we not be helped to do so by communing with our Father in the divine supernatural language of the Spirit, which He has so graciously given?

7. Praying in other tongues is a means of keeping me free from contamination by the ungodly, profane, and vulgar talk which goes on about me at my daily work, in the factory or shop, etc. As I work, I can quietly pray in tongues, (speaking to myself and to God, I Cor. 14:28) and in some way build up a wall about

me that shuts out these things, and leaves me unaffected by them. Many have learned this truth to their benefit.

A very refined lady came to us one time, saying that she had gotten work in a factory where a large number of women worked. After working a few days, she said she hardly believed that she could go back another day, because the talk around her was only profane, and vulgar, and obscene from morning till night. She said she felt almost as if she had been so contaminated by quitting time, by the filth around her, that she was filthy herself. We told her to go back the next day and just spend the day quietly communing with God, speaking in other tongues to herself and to God. A few days later she came to us and said it was wonderful what God was doing for her. She said that as soon as she started work she began praising Him quietly with other tongues, and continued to do so all day. The result was that a wall of protection seemed to be built up around her which caused the vile, filthy talk to have no effect on her at all, and when she left work at night she felt clean and refreshed, and was rejoicing in the Lord. If you, who read this, are in circumstances similar to hers, just try her method of spiritual warfare.

8. Praying in other tongues provides a way for things to be prayed for, which need prayer, but for which no one thinks to pray, or of which they know nothing. Since the Holy Spirit, and not our own mind, directs the praying in this case, He can direct it to present needs to God, of which we are entirely ignorant.

A multitude of cases could be mentioned where people have felt a burden to pray, although they did not know what it was for. In many cases it seemed that natural words were entirely inadequate to express what was felt in the heart of the one who prayed. They felt that they were not prevailing in prayer until, with reckless abandon, they threw away all thought of using their own language, and began to speak with other tongues. Soon they found that the burden began to lift and they felt that the thing for which they prayed had been accomplished. Often they have found out later, by comparing notes as to time, that someone was in desperate need or in a great danger just at the time they felt the urge to pray. Since they did not know about the need at the time, they had no way of knowing, in the natural, for what to pray. When they prayed with other tongues it gave the Holy Spirit the opportunity to direct their prayer so that it fully presented the need to God, who heard and answered.

9. "For with stammering lips and another tongue will He speak to this people. To whom He said, This is the rest wherewith ye may cause the weary to rest; and this is the refreshing: ..." (Isa. 28:11-12.) Surely in the rounds of daily life, with all the weariness and toils and cares, we need that God-given rest and refreshing. Since the mind does not direct the praying when we pray with other tongues, and since the mind does not even understand what we pray about (I Cor. 14:14), therefore, it can utterly relax and rest as we pray with our spirit; and it is truly wonderful rest and refreshing which we receive in this way. Try it yourself and you will find it gloriously true.

10. Speaking with other tongues provides the most perfect way to praise and give thanks to God. How often, as we think of His wonders, and His great love to us, there rises in our hearts such a fountain of praise that it seems our natural words utterly fail to provide an adequate channel through which its gushing waters may flow; but when we launch out into the realm of the supernatural, and begin to pray with other tongues, our hearts are satisfied, and this precious fountain of praise is fully released. "What is it then? I will pray with the spirit, and I will pray with the understanding also: I will sing with the spirit, and I will sing with the understanding also. Else when thou shalt bless with the spirit, how shall he that occupieth the room of the unlearned say Amen at thy giving of thanks, seeing he understandeth not what thou sayest? FOR THOU VERILY GIVEST THANKS WELL, but the other is not edified." (I Cor. 14:15-17.)

11. In the book of James we are told that the tongue is an unruly member, full of deadly poison, which no man can tame. (James 3:8.) Since this is true, it seems very significant to us that, when we speak with other tongues, our lips and tongue must be fully yielded to the guidance of the Spirit, and submissive to His will. If the man fully submits his tongue, the unruly member, to the guidance of the Spirit surely he has taken a long step toward fully yielding all his members to God. As he continues to do this day after day in his private devotions the habit

of yieldedness becomes more fixed in him, which is certainly a desirable result.

At this point we list a number of reasons for speaking with tongues which do not relate to our private life, but they are, nevertheless, of real importance.

First: Speaking with tongues is the Scriptural, initial, outward evidence of the receiving of the Holy Spirit. In every case in the New Testament, where it tells of people receiving the Holy Spirit, it says that they spoke with tongues, if anything at all is said about what happened, (Acts 2:4; 10:44-48; 19:6.) Since it is made clear in the Scripture that all Christians should receive the Holy Spirit, and since speaking with tongues is the first Bible evidence; therefore, it certainly is important that we should speak with tongues. When Peter heard those Gentiles (Acts 10:44-47) speak with tongues, he announced at once that they had received the Holy Spirit. Should not we be satisfied with the evidence which satisfied Peter that these Gentiles had received the Holy Spirit? Should we count anything of little value which is the Bible evidence of such a very important thing as the receiving of the blessed Holy Spirit? We leave you to answer these questions for yourself.

Second: "I would that ye all spake with tongues," (I Cor. 14:5.) This evidently is talking about bringing forth a message to be interpreted in the assembly of Christians. Certainly this lovely supernatural means of bringing inspiration and blessing to the church is not to be regarded as having no value. Why should the apostle say he wished we all would do it if there was no value there? Do we believe his words were divinely inspired by the Holy Spirit? (I Cor. 14:37.) Then let us go on to exercise this lovely gift, that the church might receive edifying by its employment in connection with the sister gift of interpretation of tongues.

Third: When rightly used, in line with the Word of God, speaking with tongues convinces the unbeliever of the reality of the power of God, and often causes him to turn to God and be saved. (I Cor. 14:22.) Almost anyone who has had any extensive contact with churches where these supernatural manifestations are expected, has seen more than one case where the unsaved have been moved to turn to God as they have seen these miracu-

lous things. If these things are kept in line with the teachings of
God's Word, they will be a source of inspiration and blessing to
all.

Fourth: Jesus said, "These signs shall follow them that believe; ... they shall speak with new tongues;" (Mark 16:17).
Are you a believer? Does He say some believers shall speak with
new tongues? I do not believe that Jesus made this statement for
nothing. I prefer to believe His Word rather than man's contrary
arguments. How about you? Also Paul said, "Forbid not to speak
with tongues." (I Cor. 14:39.)

How Can We Speak With Tongues?

There is another phase of this matter of speaking with tongues which should be discussed, if the foregoing thoughts are to
be most helpful. We assume, of course, that all recognize the
fact that no one will, or does, speak with tongues under the moving of the Holy Spirit until he has first received the Holy Spirit.
Unfortunately, but true, we have multiplied thousands of people
who have received the Holy Spirit, and spoken with other tongues
at the time they received Him, but have not clearly understood
what actually happens when a person speaks with tongues, and
have not realized the part that the man's will plays in the matter.
Unfortunately there has been an expression used which is mis-
leading, and it has caused great damage to many. Very often it
has been said, concerning speaking with tongues, "The Holy
Spirit speaks through the man." Or to someone upon whom the
Spirit was moving we have said, "Now just let the Spirit speak
through you." These expressions convey the idea that the Holy
Spirit actually *does* the speaking Himself. The fact is that this is
not true. The Holy Spirit does *not* speak. The Word plainly
teaches that the man DOES the speaking, but that the Spirit
supernaturally DIRECTS it.

A careful reading of Acts 2:4 will make this clear to the
thoughtful reader. Many of the modern translations of the New
Testament make it even more clear than the Authorized Version.
Weymouth's translation says, "They were all filled with the Holy
Spirit, and began to speak in other tongues according as the Spirit
gave them words to utter." Now what could be more plain than

that the man speaks the words which the Holy Spirit gives him to speak? The new 1941 edition put out by the Roman Catholic Church gives a beautiful rendering of this verse, which reads as follows: "And they were all filled with the Holy Spirit and began to speak in foreign tongues, even as the Holy Spirit prompted them to speak." James Moffet's translation says, "They began to speak in foreign tongues, as the Spirit enabled them to express themselves." The Concordant version renders the verse under discussion, "And they began to speak in different languages, according as the Spirit gave them to declaim." When someone is prompted, the one who is doing the prompting tells the speaker what to say, and he says it. Surely nothing could be more clear than this.

There is nothing supernatural about the fact that the man speaks with tongues. That is based on an act of will. We freely admit that very often there is a strong urge by the Spirit to speak with tongues, but still the man's will is in control. The man can stop any time he wants to, and if he knows it, he can start at any time. Then what is the miracle connected with speaking with tongues? For certainly there is a miracle involved. The miracle is not in the *fact* that the man speaks, but in *what* he speaks. As long as a man speaks with other tongues, he has absolutely no control as to *what* he says. What he speaks is entirely supernatural.

It would be foolish and useless for the Apostle Paul to give instructions in the Bible, as to when to speak with tongues, and when not to do so, if the man was unable to obey these instructions. It is made very clear in I Cor. 14 that the man controls the speaking with tongues. Notice carefully verses 14 and 15, where Paul says, "I WILL pray with the spirit, etc." Now the reason we have so many who have no freedom to pray with the spirit (other tongues) is because of the fear of "getting in the flesh," as they say. They are afraid that if they lift up their voice and speak, they will be doing something themselves which is supposed to be of the Spirit, and so they will not do it. In reality the completed manifestation of speaking in other tongues is made up of two elements. One is entirely natural; the other entirely supernatural.

Since it is completely impossible to speak two languages at the same moment, therefore the position of faith is this, that the man will cast away all thought of speaking his natural words, and will, in faith, look up and expect a supernatural moving by the Spirit which dwells within. Then, when he feels the moving of the Spirit, his step of faith is to lift his voice and begin to speak whatever sounds come, as the result of the Spirit's moving. It is none of the man's business what the sounds are which he speaks. That is God's part. The one who has real faith will trust God to do His part, that is, prompt him to form the words on his lips, and then he will lift up his voice and speak out whatever comes. This point is very important, (I have repeated this idea for emphasis). Now long experience, as pastor of one church for seventeen years, and also work in the evangelistic field, has taught me that most people will not obey these instructions. They are too completely bound to the tradition of praising the Lord in their own language. However, there are some who will think this through, and see that the position of faith is to absolutely cast aside their own words, and wait for the Spirit to prompt them, and when He does so to lift their voices and speak out whatever sounds come, with reckless indifference as to what they are. That is faith. If it is only stammering lips at first (Isa. 28-11-12), do not let that bother you in the least. Go right on praising God with these stammering sounds, and soon you will be speaking a clear language, if you will rejoice to speak whatever God puts on your lips. In fact there are many earnest souls that have not yet received the Holy Spirit, who could receive Him at once if they would follow the principles herein indicated.

Now after one follows the practice of praying with other tongues in his private prayer life for some time it becomes like second nature to him to do so. He finds that the Spirit never fails to respond to his step of faith (lifting his voice in expectation) so he does not even wait for any moving of the Spirit on his lips, but just steps out and begins to speak, knowing that the Holy Spirit will give the words which He wants him (the man) to speak. Many have testified to the writer that it has become more natural to speak with tongues, when they pray, than to speak their own natural language, and we feel that this should be the normal experience of all Spirit-filled Christians. Do not allow Satan to defeat you at this point by telling you that you are "getting in the flesh," for he will do so if he can. Where, we ask, do we find any warning in the Word of God concerning the danger of getting in the flesh in connection with receiving the Holy Spirit and speaking with other tongues? We believe most sincerely that the Lord faithfully warns his people at every point where there is danger of doing something which will hinder our spiritual progress.

Chapter VI

EVIDENCES EXPECTED IN CONNECTION WITH RECEIVING THE HOLY SPIRIT

Almost everyone who has had any thing to do with the Full Gospel (often called Pentecostal) movement has heard the following statement, either privately or in public; "You will not need anyone to tell you when you receive the Holy Spirit. If you are in doubt, then you have not received Him." After being in this movement for over twenty-five years, and seeing thousands receive the Holy Spirit, we find that we cannot agree with this statement altogether. People believe that they have, or have not, received certain experiences from God on the basis of what they have been taught that they may expect the accompanying evidences to be.

Sad, but true, multitudes have listened to the testimonies of others, forgetting what the Bible teaches, and from these testimonies they have drawn the conclusions that they must have certain physical or mental evidences to prove that they are saved, or filled with the Holy Spirit. It may be that these evidences, which they are looking for, are not according to the Word of God at all, but as long as they believe that they must have these evidences, they will not believe that they are filled with the Spirit until they have them, regardless of what other evidences they do have, which are according to Scripture.

Then again, people may not know what the Bible teaches, so they do not know how to classify the experiences they have. A few illustrations from our personal experiences will help us to see that it is of utmost importance to know just what the Bible teaches concerning any of these things, so that we may stand by faith on the promises of God.

In the summer of 1937 the writer came in contact with an old gentleman at a large camp meeting. He was standing in the back of the tabernacle between meetings, when the Spirit of the Lord began to move upon him, and he began trembling all over. He was bewildered and amazed, and did not know what to think about it. We sat down with him and explained to him what the Bible taught concerning the receiving of the Holy Spirit. Before we were finished the Spirit moved mightily upon him, and he suddenly fell prostrate on the floor and burst forth speaking in other tongues. He shouted and praised God in other tongues for a long time before ever rising up from where he was. At last he arose and then told us this remarkable story. Back in the year 1883 he had been under a great burden of sorrow for some time, and, being a Christian he had cried mightily to God for help. One day, while in prayer, the power and glory of the Lord swept over him and he began speaking a strange language he had never learned. He felt great joy, but also fear, because he could not understand what was happening. Those around him became excited and thought he had lost his mind, and being in the dark himself as to the meaning of it all, he was not sure but what they were right. He therefore cried to God, and asked Him never to let such a dreadful thing happen again. Fifty-four years passed and it did not happen again, but when he heard of the receiving of the Holy Spirit, with the accompanying sign of speaking in other tongues, he knew at once that he had received the Holy Spirit when a young man fifty-four years before. At once he began to rejoice and praise God for the blessed fullness of the Spirit, because he saw that it was according to the Word. Now all of those years he had missed the blessings he might have enjoyed because he did not know that he had received the Holy Spirit.

Another strange case will help us to see that people believe they are saved, or filled with the Spirit, when they have the evidence for which they are looking. One Sunday afternoon we were sitting in the living room of our home, talking to some friends, when we saw a beautiful car stop in front of the house. We went out on the porch to meet the man who got out of the car, and saw that he was a total stranger. When greetings were exchanged he told us that a man in a town thirty miles away had told him to come to us, and that we would help him, and he would receive the Holy Spirit. One could see, even then, the tears standing in his eyes, he was so hungry to be filled with the

Spirit. We invited him in, and told him that most certainly he would receive. quoting to him Luke 11:13, "If ye then, being evil, know how to give good gifts to your children: how much more shall your heavenly Father give the Holy Spirit to them that ask Him?" He came in and took a chair offered him, and we began to discuss what the Word teaches concerning the receiving of the Holy Spirit. After we had spent an hour in the Word, we told him just to look up in faith as we laid hands on him. At once the Spirit fell upon him and he began to shake so violently that we were afraid our chair would be broken to pieces (he being a large man). His arms were swinging and jerking like the wind tossed branches of a tree, and stammering sounds were coming out of his mouth. We gently pushed his arms down and said, "Brother, let this energy out in speaking, as God intends, rather than in all this shaking." Suddenly he relaxed his muscles and burst forth at once speaking a beautiful language, and for more than an hour shouted in other tongues so loudly that he could be heard a long distance.

At last he ceased and took his departure, still praising and glorifying God. We did not see him again for a week, and then had only a few minutes to talk with him. After that we saw him no more for eight months, when one Sunday evening he came into our church, and when opportunity was given, he rose to testify. This is about what he said, "I want to confess my sin of unbelief to God, and to Brother Stiles, and these people. Eight months ago I came to your pastor's house, and while there the Spirit fell on me, and I spoke fluently in other tongues for an hour or more, but before I got across the street to my car, when leaving, the devil whispered to me that I had not received the Holy Spirit, because I had not fallen prostrate on the floor, as I had seen others do. I was foolish enough to believe him, and therefore did not testify to others that I had received the Holy Spirit. I had no joy, because it is the assurance that the Holy Spirit is abiding within which brings the joy. I have been in doubt and discouragement all this time. This afternoon, while a group of us were praying out on a hill top, a young lady laid hands on me, and I burst forth speaking in tongues again, for the first time in eight months, and God severely rebuked me for not believing I had received the Holy Spirit, when I had the clear Scriptural evidence which the apostles had. From now on I shall believe the Word, rather than looking for the experiences of others."

You see, this man had received the Holy Spirit, but would not believe it because he did not have the experience he expected. He was not willing to go by the Word of God. He wanted other proof.

Still another case might help along this line. One of our oldest and best known ministers, who has gone to his heavenly reward, told us the following: In the early days of this blessed outpouring of the Holy Spirit, there were two missions in the large city in which he lived where this Full Gospel message was being preached, and where people were receiving the Holy Spirit, and speaking with other tongues. In one of these missions practically everyone who received the Spirit fell prostrate on the floor before beginning to speak with other tongues. In the other mission almost no one fell prostrate, but practically everyone in this mission, who received the Spirit, gave forth interpretations of tongues, concerning the return of the Lord, in addition to speaking with other tongues. "Now," said he, "How do you explain this strange situation?" He felt, as well as we, that the only explanation of what he saw was this: the people received what they expected. They believed the leaders were godly men, and they were; but they taught their people to expect different evidences. After all, we get what we really have faith to receive. Now this brother's wife received the Holy Spirit in the mission where no one fell prostrate, but all gave interpretations. She, like the others, did not fall prostrate, nor did she give interpretations, as she was supposed to do. This troubled her greatly, and Satan used it to torment her for some time, and caused her to doubt that she had received the Holy Spirit, although she spoke with other tongues fluently. She finally saw that the Bible evidence was the speaking with other tongues, and when she took her position on the Word of God, she had peace and never doubted again that she was Spirit-filled. Later she received the gift of interpretation of tongues and used it to the glory of God.

Let us remember that it is believing God's Word, and acting upon it, which brings the blessing, and makes us pleasing in God's sight. (Heb. 11:6.) Let us follow this matter a little farther. Among Spirit-filled people everywhere the great joy which they had at the time they received the Holy Spirit is emphasized. The fact is that they make it appear, by their testimony, that the great joy they received, rather than the speaking with other tongues, was the proof that they had received the Holy Spirit. Testimonies of this kind leave the impression with the seeker that necessarily he must have great joy at the time he first speaks with tongues, or he will not believe he has received the Holy Spirit. We have gone to a number of people who testified thus, and asked them this question, "Did you have the great joy of which you speak, right at the time you first spoke with other tongues?" In various cases the answer has been, "Well now, let me see. You know, when I think of it, it was about three days (or one day or two weeks) after I first spoke with tongues that the great joy came." In other words, when they were willing to take the Word for it, and thank God for the heavenly gift, because they had the Bible evidence, then the joy came. Joy is a human reaction to faith. You have the joy of salvation when you believe that you are saved. We have said to these people, "Why don't you tell the truth when you testify, and relate your experience as it actually was, so as not to leave a wrong impression with other seekers? You freely admit, when questioned carefully, that you did not get the great joy you speak of until sometime after you received the Holy Spirit, for you did actually receive the Holy Spirit when you first spoke with other tongues." Recently in a fairly large meeting, where there were dozens who had received the Holy Spirit, the writer asked this question, "How many of you people did not have great joy right at the time that you received the Holy Spirit, and first spoke with other tongues?" In this case more than half of the Spirit-filled people in the audience testified that the great joy connected with receiving the Spirit did not come until some time after they first spoke with other tongues. What a joy to have the assurance from God's Word that we are filled with the Holy Spirit, standing on that, and that alone. Since this time we have asked the same question in many audiences, and always there has been a large number who give the same testimony.

The writer has seen many cases, and very godly people too, who would speak with tongues, but did not at the moment have great joy. Therefore they would not believe, and hence had no joy or confidence later. The experience of the writer's wife may help us. She had been seeking for some time, when one night in our own home on the farm the Spirit of the Lord moved upon her, and she began to speak with other tongues, as the Spirit gave utterance. There were only a few people gathered to pray, among them a man who had received the Holy Spirit. (You see we were in the Methodist Church at that time, and hardly knew there was a Full Gospel movement.) We were just a group of hungry people who had heard that we could receive the Holy Spirit, and we were determined to do so.

After she had spoken with tongues, she stopped and said, "Lord, I want to be sure I am filled with the Spirit." She was speaking with tongues, but had none of the joy she had expected. This man, guided by the Spirit, I am sure, said, "Sister, who is causing you to speak those words you are speaking?" Her answer was, "The Holy Spirit, I suppose." "Then," said he, "What more evidence do you want?" This conversation was repeated several times till finally she said, "Lord, I thank you. I believe I have received the Holy Spirit because I have the Bible evidence." She went to bed greatly disappointed, because she had not received what she expected. The following day she began speaking with tongues again. This time God just emptied Heaven on her, it seemed, and she was almost beside herself with joy. She ran from room to room shouting with other tongues, so filled with glory she could hardly contain it. Then out into the chicken pen she went, and stood there quite awhile shouting at the chickens with other tongues. Such glory flooded her that no words could express it. Now here is the important part of this incident. If she had not believed God's Word, and praised Him for the Gift of the Holy Spirit the night before, when she felt no joy, she would not have had the glorious experience just recorded. God honored her for accepting His Word, and believing it, and acting upon it.

To illustrate this point we recount an experience we had a

good number of years ago. Two young ladies who had been members of our church for years, had moved to another city some fifteen miles away, where they became affiliated with a local church. They were thoroughly clear in their understanding that the Holy Spirit is received by faith, so they sometimes brought seekers out to their old church for help. One time they brought a middle aged lady out, who said she wanted to receive the Holy Spirit. This was on a regular prayer meeting night, so after the meeting we laid hands on this lady, and, after waiting a short time the Spirit moved on her, and she began speaking with tongues. She went on speaking for some time, and we supposed that she felt sure that she had received the Holy Spirit. The three ladies left in their car for home, and we felt rejoiced that we had been able to help the stranger. The next morning one of the young ladies called on the long distance phone and told me the following. "When we got nearly to Miss M's place, we said to her, 'Isn't it wonderful that you received the Holy Spirit tonight?' 'Why, I didn't receive the Holy Spirit' she replied'." The two were so astonished at her answer that one called me the next day as I have stated. When she told me this over the phone I at once replied that she did receive the Holy Spirit, and that I would prove it to her. I realized that here was another case of Satan talking someone out of what they have. I immediately changed my plans for the morning, and dressed and drove down to the apartment house which she managed. I was really angry at Satan for cheating a child of God out of her rightful heritage, and I knew we must take a strong stand against him. I went up the apartment steps about three at a time, and pushing the door open I found Sister M in the entrance hall, with a dust mop in one hand and a pail in the other. At once I said to her, "You told the girls last night that you did not receive the Holy Spirit. You did; and I'll prove it to you." She replied, "Well, I-I-I didn't feel as I expected I would feel, if I received the Holy Spirit." "Well now, that is something different; but you did have the Bible evidence of speaking with other tongues, so you did receive the Holy Spirit." There was an old fashioned hall tree in the entrance hall with a seat, and I said, "Put down that mop and bucket, and kneel down right there, and you are going to speak with tongues again." She obeyed, and dropped on her knees by the seat, at the same time looking up with expectancy. We laid our hands on her and she began to speak with tongues at once. We were kneeling right where any of the apartment renters would have to pass by us, if they went in or out, but I was fighting the devil, and I did not care. We knelt for a long time, and she kept speaking louder and louder, and with more freedom all the time. It wasn't long until a free clear language was just flowing out and you could see by the look on her face that she was getting the joy and glory in her soul. Finally she arose and I said, "Now, do you feel as you expected to feel when receiving the Holy Spirit?" "I surely do," she replied, and from then on she was sure she had received the Holy Spirit.

Her pastor told me later that she was always a rather depressed soul that looked down, rather than up, and she had been seeking the Holy Spirit for a long time, and was greatly discouraged. When she entered the church the Sunday after receiving the Spirit, he said he knew at once that something dynamic had happened. Her head was up, and she was walking with a new spring in her step. As soon as she had an opportunity she testified that she had received the Holy Spirit, and so far as I know, has never doubted in the years that have intervened.

Now if I had left her alone, and not followed her to her home, she would have gone on in discouragement, taking the position that she had not received the Holy Spirit. This happened near Christmas and a few days later I received a letter from her telling me that she was sending me a New Testament in commemoration of her receiving the Holy Spirit. This Testament is now badly worn out, and has been replaced by a lovely new one given by a church where we told the story of Miss M and showed the Testament.

Now it would be a mistake to leave people with the idea that all will be joyous after they have received the Holy Spirit, and have had the joy of assurance that He is abiding within. As soon as Jesus received the Holy Spirit, after His baptism in the Jordan River, He was led of the Spirit into the wilderness to be tempted of the devil; and it has been the experience of many, that they have been beset with trials and temptations right after they received the Spirit, such as they have never known before. However, they have a new power with which to meet these temptations, which, if employed as God intended, will bring them out more than conqueror. The writer's wife, after that glorious experience already recorded, was allowed by God to have a wilderness experience in which she was tempted beyond any limits which she had ever known before. Satan tried every way possible to get her to doubt, even the very deity of Jesus Christ. His attacks were so subtle and continuous that it was almost unbearable at times, but, thank God, the Lord kept directing her to the Word as her source of defense. This testing lasted forty days, before it was lifted, and for more than twenty years she has never had a doubt concerning these things.

Now we are not suggesting that all will have such a testing, but we do want to warn people that the Holy Spirit was not given that they might have joyful ease all the time, but that they might have divine supernatural power to meet the onslaughts of the enemy of our souls, for it is by meeting the enemy and conquering him in the Spirit, that we grow spiritually and become more like our Lord.

There is another angle from which we may look at this matter, which will help us to see that the Bible evidence is the only evidence we need to prove that we have received the Holy Spirit. We have met many people, and very godly people too, who very determinedly contend that they have received the Holy Spirit, and still they have not had the evidence of speaking with other tongues, as the Spirit gives utterance. Now these are good and honest people, but they do not see that the Bible teaches that other tongues is the scriptural evidence. Many of them have had wonderful experiences with God, and take the position that these experiences prove their claim to have received the Holy Spirit. One sister who was a preacher, and a godly consecrated woman, told us that she knew she had received the Holy Spirit, because she had lain for many hours prostrate under the power of the Spirit, and that during this time she had a vision of King David. We often have wondered how she knew her vision was of King David. Now if we cared to be a little hard on her theories, we might have asked her to point out the Scripture which said that one would have a vision of David as an evidence of the receiving of the Holy Spirit. Let us be satisfied WITH NO LESS, AND DEMAND NO MORE, than the Bible evidence of speaking with other tongues, as the Spirit gives utterance.

In reading Acts 10:44-47 we see that the speaking with other tongues was the thing which proved to Peter that the people at the house of Cornelius had received the Holy Spirit. Even though he had previously believed that the benefits of God, and His great salvation, were not for Gentiles; still he did not hesitate to announce that they had received the Holy Spirit as soon as he heard them speak with tongues. There is no example in the Bible where they waited to see how the supposed recipient subsequently behaved before announcing that they had received the Holy Spirit. No; as soon as they heard them speak with other tongues, they announced that they had received the Spirit. Shall we not take the position with Peter, rather than with those who follow men's traditions?

Another experience of the writer might be helpful. We were invited, while still acting as pastor of the church which we served for so many years, to go and hold a revival in a small mountain town in another state. Very soon after beginning the meeting the people began to receive the Holy Spirit in considerable numbers, especially was there a moving among the children. In this meeting there was a young man who was greatly blessed and he said to us; "How I wish my mother might be here." When asked where she was he told us she was about thirty miles away in another town. We told him that we would provide a place for her to stay a few days if he would take his car and go and get her. This he did, and she came gladly, as she loved the Lord sincerely. She had never had the opportunity to go to school, having been brought up in the back woods, and so could not read nor write. Naturally her vocabulary was limited, and it was difficult to get certain ideas into her mind, but we did the best we could to use simple language which she would understand. At the end of the first service she came forward and sat on the front seat with others to receive the Holy Spirit. Almost at once there was a moving of the Spirit upon her, and when we laid hands on her it was much increased, but she would not speak at all. Her lips were

moving rapidly, forming words which were prompted by the Holy
Spirit, but she would not do her part, and lift her voice to speak
them. We tried every way to get her to speak, but all to no avail.
She would just sit and shake, but would not make a sound.
Finally, after we had done all we knew to help her see that she
must do the speaking by an act of the will, she opened her eyes,
looking right at us, and said, "No, not yet, not yet. I ain't clear
out yet, and I know when I'm out." Now she was expecting that
the Lord was going to make her completely unconscious, and
while in that condition, He was going to speak through her vocal
organs. We have often wondered how she expected to know
that she spoke with tongues if she was to be unconscious while it
was going on. When we finally got her to see what her part was
she began speaking with tongues and rejoiced greatly in it. We
believe that you, who read this, would be greatly surprised to
know that many people have come to us, after receiving the Holy
Spirit, and said in wonder, and amazement, "Why brother, I
was conscious all the time."

I believe that not many preachers have taught people that
they would be unconscious when receiving the Holy Spirit, but
certainly many people have gotten that idea from some source.
Probably, when they have seen people lying prostrate, they have
had the idea that they were unconscious, and therefore have expected to be unconscious themselves.

We might give many other illustrations to prove that the
expecting of other evidences than the scriptural one (speaking
with tongues) has kept many godly people from believing they
have received the Holy Spirit, and has thus kept them from
greater blessings and usefulness to God. Reader, go by the Bible.
Don't let anyone tell you that you have not received the Holy
Spirit, when you have the clear Bible evidence, (speaking with
tongues) even though you may speak very little at that time.
Any speaking with tongues at all is proof of the presence of the
Holy Spirit, just as much as if you spoke fluently. Take the
position that you have received the Holy Spirit, but that you are
going to go right on until the speaking becomes as natural as
talking your own natural language. That will soon come if you
will use what has already been given you with which to praise

Him, regardless of what it sounds like. So often we have seen people speak with tongues a little bit, and those around have said, "Too bad, sister, you did not receive tonight." And what has been the result? The sister has gone home discouraged and disappointed, feeling that she must start at the bottom and laboriously climb up again. The actual fact was that the Holy Spirit was in her just as much as He ever would be, but she had not yet learned how to yield fully to His movings upon her.

Chapter VII

FEARS THAT HINDER

Almost every one who has seen the blessed truth that we may receive the Holy Spirit today, accompanied by the Bible evidence of speaking with other tongues, has been hindered at some point in seeking and receiving Him, by fears of one kind or another. Not only the seeker has been hindered, but multitudes have been kept from enjoying blessed freedom in the Spirit after they have received Him because of these fears. All such fears are the result of wrong teaching, or lack of teaching as to what is in God's Word. We purpose, in the following pages, to discuss some of these fears, with the hope that those bound by them may be set free.

One of the first of these to assail the person who has recently come to know that he can receive the Holy Spirit, is the fear that he may get a false experience. Satan always has a representative ready to tell awful tales about how someone sought for the Holy Spirit, and became devil possessed. Usually the story has passed through several hands, and is only hearsay, but it plants fears in the mind of the seeker that very often are most difficult to get rid of. He hears accounts of how someone, somewhere, was cursing God in a foreign language, when he was supposed to be speaking with other tongues. Then people have often been strongly urged by preachers to come and seek the Holy Spirit, but almost in the same breath they are warned to be careful and not "get in the flesh," or they might get something false or spurious. To the fortunate person who has escaped these things they may seem of little importance, but not so to those who have fallen a prey to them. Here is a person who desires with all his heart to follow God, and he sees clearly that he ought to receive the Holy Spirit. He begins waiting on God, and at once Satan is right there to remind him of these fears which have been planted in his heart. People cannot realize the awful mental and spiritual anguish that others go through, when assailed by this fear, until they have experienced it themselves. Many have been so frightened by what they have seen or heard, that they have turned back altogether, and given up the thought of receiving the Spirit. They know there is such a thing as demon possession, and they also know that Satan does supernatural things. How can they be sure that these terrible things they have heard of will not happen to them? Some denominations flatly state that speaking with other tongues is of the devil, and, without doubt, there are many godly Christian people in these groups. With so many ready to plant fears, and some of them godly, but mistaken people, surely the earnest seeker should have some solid ground from the Scripture on which to stand. He cannot look to God with real faith as long as he is beset with these fears.

One of the best Scriptures to quiet his fears of getting a false experience, or a wrong spirit, is Luke 11:11-13. Here it is emphatically shown that a natural human father would not give a son a worthless or harmful substitute when he asked for good food, and then goes on to say, "If ye then, being evil, know how to give good gifts unto your children: how much more shall your heavenly Father give the Holy Spirit to them that ask Him?" What thinking person, if he stops to consider, could believe that a loving God would allow Satan to give him something false and harmful, when he is earnestly seeking to be filled with the Holy Spirit according to His commandment?

Let us remember also that if there was any danger of getting something false and harmful, surely the Lord would warn us of that danger. We should know that a loving God would faithfully warn His children at any point where there is a real danger. A good Scripture to stand on is I John 5:-14-15, "And this is the confidence that we have in Him, that, if we ask any thing according to His will, He heareth us: and if we know that He hear us, whatsoever we ask, we know that we have the petitions that we desired of Him." We know that it is God's will that we should receive the Holy Spirit (Eph. 5:18), and that we should not receive anything false or harmful. Therefore, we can come to Him with absolute confidence. How dishonoring it is to God to think that He would allow His children to receive something false or harmful, when they come earnestly seeking His best. Remember the promise, "No good thing will He withhold from them that walk uprightly." (Psalm 84:11) Let us honor God by believing in His love and goodness. It is a direct insult to Him; when we suggest that He is not wise, loving, and powerful enough to protect His seeking children from getting anything false or harmful.

Another fear is the fear that I will get "IN THE FLESH," as it is often expressed. By this the person means that he will do something of his own will, and through his natural faculties, which is supposed to be supernatural and of the Spirit. Let us state right here that there is no warning in the Bible that such a danger exists in connection with receiving the Holy Spirit, and speaking with other tongues. Surely Satan is a master hand at building up hindrances, in the minds of God's children, to keep them from a walk of real faith and confidence, and he often uses other children of God to accomplish his purposes. Now let us look at the evil results that come from this fear. Since most seekers for the Holy Spirit have had the idea that the Spirit will speak through them (This is a mistaken idea. See chapter "Why Speak With Tongues?") they are afraid to lift up their voices and speak when the Spirit puts supernatural words on their lips. As soon as they find that in the speaking, they are doing something which they can control, by an act of will, they often stop at once, as Satan suggests to them that they are getting "in the flesh." We have found many people who have been seeking the Holy Spirit for years, and many times the Spirit has moved upon their lips to form words, but this fear has kept them from speaking with other tongues, as He is trying to get them to do. Their very conscientiousness is the thing which is hindering them. They are so anxious to be sure that they do not do something in the flesh, which is supposed to be of the Spirit, that they will not do anything; and yet there is very definitely a part for the man to perform by an act of the will. One dear elderly sister told the writer that she had been earnestly seeking the Holy Spirit for twenty-nine years, but had not received Him. When we explained to her that she must lift her voice and speak the words which the Spirit put on her lips, she at once began to speak a beautiful, clear

language. Two years later she told us of the wonderful fellowship she was having with the Spirit; and she also told us that she
never would have received Him, if someone had not shown her
that she must do the speaking with other tongues. She was expecting the Holy Spirit to "speak through her;" (an unscriptural
term) and fears that she would do that which He was supposed
to do, had frustrated her every attempt to receive Him. Her pastor told us that she was the most godly, prayerful saint in his
church, and still she had been hindered all those years from
enjoying the blessed fellowship of the Spirit through fears that
had come because of lack of knowledge as to what the Bible
teaches.

Now this fear of getting in the flesh has hindered not only
those who are seeking to receive the Holy Spirit, but also those
who have already received Him. They are afraid to speak with
other tongues in their private prayer life, as the Bible teaches
every Spirit-filled saint should do. There is yet another place
where this fear hinders. Many people have been hindered from
bringing forth messages in tongues and interpretations, or messages in prophecy, when the Spirit was trying to get them to do
these things, because they feared they would be getting in the
flesh if they went ahead by an act of the will. The real truth is
that the manifestation of these gifts (tongues, interpretation of
tongues and prophecy) lies entirely within the province of the
man's will. A careful study of I Cor. 14 will make this clear to
any earnest reader of the Word. Here the Apostle Paul gives
many instructions concerning the use of these gifts, and it is
utterly unthinkable that the Holy Spirit would inspire him to
give instructions which the man was unable to obey. Notice
particularly verse 32, "And the spirits of the prophets are subject
to the prophets." As a result of this fear, many have allowed
these lovely inspirational gifts to lie dormant for years, thus
reducing their usefulness in the body of Christ, and also they
are missing the spiritual upbuilding which would have resulted
from their use.

At this point many might be confused if there were not some
further explanation. They might justifiably ask the question, if
the control of these gifts lies in the power of the man's will, then

where does the supernatural element come in? Surely we would
not want any one to believe that these precious gifts are purely
natural; for they are not, but still we must insist that their operation is under the control of the human will. Just here we will
be helped by explaining some of the miracles in the Bible. Possibly you, who are reading this, have never stopped to consider
that the man, who had a part with God in bringing about a
miracle, always made the first move. Take for instance, the
miracles of Moses, Elijah, Elisha and others, and let us see how
they were brought about. Moses stretched out his rod over the
Red Sea, and then the water separated, and they went over on
dry ground. (Exodus 14:16-21.) Elijah struck the water of Jordan
and it opened for him and Elisha to pass over (II Kings 2:8).
Elisha threw salt in the water of Jericho, and pronounced that
the waters were healed, and it was true that they were (II Kings
2:21-22). He cut a stick and threw it on the water where the axe
head had fallen, and the axe head floated to the surface (II Kings
6:6-7). Now we ask the question: was there anything supernatural about those initial moves which the man made? No;
they were all entirely natural. They were acts of the will, without
which the miracles never would have come to pass. Each of
these acts constituted a step of FAITH, and God honors real
faith whenever He sees it. In some cases the Lord told the man
to do the thing he did, but in most cases there is no such record.
In either case it lay within the power of the man's will to take,
or not to take, the initial step which brought about the miracle.
When once we see that these supernatural things are brought
about by a step of faith which we can take, by an act of will,
the mystery connected with them is quite largely taken away,
and the fear of doing something which we should not do is entirely removed. Why not go by the Book in these things, instead
of going by hearsay and tradition?

Another fear which is most real to many, especially the very
conscientious, is the fear of being a hypocrite. Satan will use
this as a means to keep these people from speaking with tongues
in their private prayer life after they have received the Holy
Spirit, and thus they will be deprived of the spiritual upbuilding
which would result from it. He will tell them that they are not

good enough to be speaking with tongues, and that if they do it when they have imperfections in their lives, they will be hypocrites. He suggests to them that they are trying to appear more spiritual than they are, and that this is an awful sin. He even will whisper to them that it is blasphemy against the Holy Spirit to speak with tongues unless they are living in complete victory, and he sets the standard for them at a level of spiritual development to which he knows they have not yet attained. Thus one of the powerful means of gaining spiritual strength, and reaching the level of spiritual life, and victory, which their hearts desire, is denied to them. Now all of these fears can be traced back to a very few fundamental errors in the minds of people. The most detrimental error is the belief that the Holy Spirit is given on the basis of our personal holiness, and therefore, when we do receive Him, it is proof of holiness in our lives. Also it is largely believed among people that speaking with tongues, and the manifesting of other gifts of the Spirit, is an evidence of a high degree of Christian character. Nothing could be much farther from the truth. In other parts of this book we have shown, both from the Bible, and from the experiences of people, that many have manifested real spiritual gifts while living far below the spiritual level which God would have them maintain. Are we, therefore, to be denied the use of these means of grace because some have misused them and lived in a way dishonoring to God? Are we saying we will have nothing to do with shotguns because some people have misused them to kill some other person? Let us remember that the possession of spiritual gifts, or a shotgun, lays on us an added responsibility to live right, for they are dangerous if we possess them, and do not live as we should. Now we would not wish the reader to get the idea that they should stop seeking or manifesting spiritual gifts because others have misused them. The Word of God still says to covet earnestly the gifts of the Spirit, (I Cor. 12:31; 14:1) and surely we should obey it, if we are to grow into the likeness of Christ. Let us also remind the reader that if God waited for perfect people to use in these things, He never would use anyone. If we would keep ever before us the fact that these gifts of the Spirit are provided for God's children, as one of the means of their spiritual development, we would be looking at them in the right light. Paul says in Romans 1:11, "For I long to see you, that I may impart unto you some spiritual gift, to the end ye may be established." Any sincere Christian who has been hindered from receiving the Holy Spirit and praying with other tongues, by the fear of being a hypocrite, should realize that this is only a clever ruse of Satan to hold back their spiritual progress.

A fear, which is closely allied to the fear of getting a false spirit, or an experience which is not genuine, is the fear of getting "tongues" without getting the Holy Spirit. Time after time preachers have stated from the platform that it is possible for Christians to get tongues, and not get the Holy Spirit, when they are seeking Him. We would like to ask these "doubt builders" to point out the Scripture upon which they base such statements. We wish they would stop and consider the spiritual devastation they cause in the lives of their hearers by saying such things.

If the Christian who has not yet received the Holy Spirit, is led to believe that he may get tongues, and still not receive the Holy Spirit, he is at once thrown into a state of confusion concerning the whole matter. How can he be sure that he has received the Spirit, if he cannot rely on the Bible evidence as being the definite proof of his having received Him? If such a thing as a saved man getting tongues without receiving the Holy Spirit were possible, why doesn't the Bible warn us of such a danger?

We notice in Acts 10:44-48 that when Peter heard these Gentiles speaking with tongues, whom he believed were not eligible to receive the Spirit, he at once said, without hesitation, that they had received the Holy Spirit as well as himself and the six Jewish Christians which were with him. If it were possible for Christians to receive tongues, and not receive the Holy Spirit, then surely here was a good place for it to happen, because these people were not even saved when Peter arrived there. They were believers in God, and the Jewish religion, but the angel who told Cornelius to send and fetch Peter, told him also that Peter would tell them words by which he and his house would be saved (Acts 11:14). Why didn't Peter take the position that he would watch these Gentiles, who had spoken with tongues, for about six months, before he could definitely say that they really had received the Holy Spirit?

Any person who is of a timid, cautious, nature would at once be put in a position where he could not seek the Holy Spirit with confidence and assurance. In fact, it would stop any logical thinker from starting out to seek the Holy Spirit, if he believed this false idea to be true. Since there is no other scriptural, initial evidence of the believer's having received the Spirit, how, we ask, would he have any way of knowing, by the Word, that he had received Him? We recognize that people have in their minds, many evidences which they believe prove that they have received the Spirit, but these are traditional and imaginary, but certainly not scriptural. If the writer's wife, who is very conservative, had had the slightest idea that a person might receive tongues, without having received the Spirit, she certainly would never have started seeking Him.

Surely we should be careful about the ideas which we pass on to others, and know that we are on scriptural ground, before we make statements which may undermine their faith, and fill their hearts with fear. Let us never be guilty of making a statement that is as unscriptural as the statement that Christians may get tongues and not receive the Holy Spirit (Luke 11:11-13).

There is another fear which is quite common, although not as destructive as the ones already mentioned. It is the fear of doing queer or unseemly things in the presence of other people. Many have been so bound by this fear, that they felt it was impossible for them to lift their voices and speak, when the Spirit moved upon them. Now, in the first place, we do not believe that the Spirit makes people do unseemly or immodest things. We recognize that it has been quite largely believed among Full Gospel people that God makes them do foolish and ridiculous things in connection with receiving the Holy Spirit, in order to properly humble them. This we do not believe to be true. We never find Jesus deliberately placing anyone, who was seeking God, in an embarrassing position, or doing that which would humiliate them. We admit that the people on the Day of Pentecost were accused of being drunk, but there is a great difference between being so joyful that they seemed almost beside themselves, and being forced to do foolish or immodest things. Of course the natural (unsaved) man often says that just speaking with other tongues is senseless and valueless, but we know that "the natural man receiveth not the things of the Spirit of God: for they are foolishness unto him: neither can he know them, because they are spiritually discerned." (I Cor. 2:14)

We believe that the Holy Spirit is gentle, like the dove which symbolized Him at the baptism of Jesus, and that true manifestations of His presence will be dignified, powerful, and convincing to the unlearned and the unbeliever. Many have seemed to take delight in seeing people do those things which embarrassed and humiliated them, but, on the whole, we have found these things to be hindrances to the best spiritual development of the individuals involved, and surely they have turned away many honest, hungry, seekers from this blessed Spirit-filled life. The reason that people delighted in these demonstrations, often violent, and sometimes unseemly and immodest, was that they believed them to be indications of the seeker's being brought into a condition of yieldedness to God. Just the reverse is true. They are indications that the seeker is not yielding to God. If he yielded fully there would be no struggles as the Spirit took up His abode in the individual's body. God's Word says in regard to the speaking with tongues, "This is the rest wherewith ye may cause the weary to rest; and this is the refreshing . . ." (Isa. 28:12). Since it is the body which is the temple of the Holy Spirit, and since the body is controlled by the mind, therefore, if the person is correctly instructed as to what constitutes yielding to the Spirit, there will be no struggling and violent demonstrations. Of the many hundreds who have received the Holy Spirit in our meetings in the last few years, almost none has given vent to such physical demonstrations, or falling prostrate on the floor.

Now if we want to help these people, who are bound by this fear of doing something unseemly in the presence of others, we would do well to have them go to a separate room, apart from people, where they will not have others curiously watching them, when they come to receive the Holy Spirit. Although many have opposed this idea, saying it is good for the person to be humiliated and embarrassed in the presence of others, we are convinced that this is not correct. We find that these people can abandon themselves to the moving of the Spirit much more freely when they are in comparative privacy, and then, after receiving Him, they become less self-conscious in the presence of others. The following incident will illustrate this truth most clearly:

We were holding services in a certain city and the blessing of the Lord was very marked. One day, after the meeting had progressed for several weeks, a very cultured, refined, lady came to us saying that she was so bound by the fear of others, that it was impossible to give even a short testimony, or lead in prayer. From appearances, she would have fainted if she had been forced to stand up in a public meeting and try to testify. We told her to come to meeting early the next evening, that we might discuss the matter privately with her, and if possible help her past this difficulty. We found, on questioning her, that she had received the Holy Spirit about two years previously, but had not spoken with other tongues since that time. We believed that this was the point at which to begin, so we had her kneel down and wait quietly for a moving of the Spirit. Soon He began to move, in response to her faith, and we laid hands on her. Since there were no curious on-lookers we were able, by a little encouragement, to get her to do her part, and begin to speak out the words the Spirit was putting on her lips. At first it was very subdued, but soon she gained confidence and was speaking freely. The blessing began to flood her soul, and at once she was so taken up with the Lord, and His blessing, that she was lost to all that was around her. From then on it would not have made any difference how many people were looking on. Soon it was time for the meeting to begin, and we went down stairs to the auditorium. She was so full that she was actually intoxicated with the mighty power of the Spirit within her. (See Eph. 5:18.) While she was in this condition of ecstasy, rejoicing in the Spirit's moving, we called upon her to testify; a thing which she never could do before. She stood to her feet and gave a good testimony, although rather faltering, but the bondage of fear was broken. The next night we gave the opportunity to testify, and she was on her feet at once, with complete freedom to speak before others. From that time on her fear was entirely a thing of the past. If we want to be the most helpful to these timid souls, let us deal with them in private, rather than taking the attitude that they can either receive the Spirit with others, or go without Him. Very often the result of taking such a position is to close the door of blessing in their faces, and keep them back from spiritual growth and development.

We cannot go into a discussion of all the fears that hinder people from receiving the Holy Spirit, but if you, who read these pages, will cast aside any idea or theory that does not definitely line up with the Word of God, you will have gone a long way toward complete deliverance from hindering fears.

Chapter VIII

RECEIVING THE HOLY SPIRIT
In the Early Church

There probably is no minister in the Full Gospel ranks who will not stand solidly for the fact that he is doing his best to pattern his work after that of the apostles of Jesus, and that he is trying to build a church as nearly as possible like the early apostolic church. We are in full harmony with this program, believing that no better can be had. Now if we want to know how to deal in the best way with those who are anxious to receive the Holy Spirit, then it seems to us that we should study very carefully how they were dealt with in the early apostolic church.

There is one point, however, which must be cleared up right at the outset, if we are to be logical in our thinking along this line. The question is this: when did the church have its beginning? We believe that almost all will agree that it came into being on the Day of Pentecost, when the disciples of Jesus received the Holy Spirit. Before that time He (the Holy Spirit) was not here on earth that all might receive Him; but from that day to this He has been here, and is now ready to enter any hungry heart.

Now Jesus' last commission to His disciples was to tarry in Jerusalem until they had received the Holy Spirit, bringing power from on high, but let us remember that this commission of Jesus was given, and carried out, before the beginning of this church age, or dispensation of the Holy Spirit. The descent of the Holy Spirit on the Day of Pentecost was the event dividing the dispensations. Let us say in passing that their tarrying was not primarily a matter of preparing themselves to receive the Holy Spirit, but it was a case of waiting for an appointed time. Notice Acts 2:1 does not say, "When the waiting ones were fully prepared, the Holy Spirit came," but it says, "When the Day of Pentecost was fully come." The coming of the Spirit was dispensational in character. He could not have come before the time appointed of God. Remember also that only Jews received the Holy Spirit on the Day of Pentecost.

Now let us examine how people were dealt with in the early church concerning the receiving of the Holy Spirit, remembering that Pentecost was the dividing line between the dispensations. Therefore we must take as our pattern those things which happened in the early church age (that is after Pentecost). As we look through the history of the early church in the Book of Acts, we find that there are four recorded cases where people were declared to have received the Holy Spirit. Let us carefully examine each one of them and see what we can learn.

Before taking up the first of these cases, however, it would be well to look at Peter's statement in Acts 2:38-39, "Then Peter said unto them, Repent, and be baptized every one of you in the name of Jesus Christ for the remission of sins, and ye shall receive the gift of the Holy Ghost. For the promise is unto you, and to your children, and to all that are afar off, even as many as the Lord our God shall call." We will observe the order of events which should take place in the experience of one who really wants to follow God; they are, Repent, be Baptized, RECEIVE the Gift of the Holy Ghost. That statement makes clear the plan for the church age. The word which is of particular interest to us at this point is GIFT.

A gift is something which cannot be earned by work, because the moment we begin to work for it, it ceases to be a gift and becomes wages, or a reward for labor. If we get it because we have done something good or meritorious, then it is a reward for merit. Now the giving of the Holy Spirit was just another demonstration of the grace of God. He freely gave, not because we were worthy, but because of His loving kindness, and our great need. We are no more worthy to receive the Holy Spirit than we are to receive salvation. Both are gracious gifts, to a needy world, from a loving God. Let us read Luke 11:13, "If ye then, being evil, know how to give good gifts unto your children: how much more shall your heavenly Father give the Holy Spirit to them that ask Him?" In the Word the receiving of the Holy Spirit is placed, as we see, on the basis of gift. Here it says your Father will GIVE the Holy Spirit. This was spoken before Pentecost. After Pentecost the thought of giving is never mentioned. The Holy Spirit was given, once for all, at that time. From then on it was a matter of the man receiving, not God giving the Spirit.

The first case of people receiving the Holy Spirit in the early church is recorded in Acts 8, verses 14 to 19. Before reading these verses let us remind the reader of what had gone before. Philip, one of the seven deacons, upon whom the apostles had laid hands, had gone to Samaria, and began to preach Christ to the people. At once a great revival started, attended by many miracles, and signs, and wonders, which were so notable that the whole city was stirred. Let us remember that these people were not Gentiles, but were of the stock of Israel (John 4:12). We shall have reason to refer to this fact later. Now let us read verses 14 to 19 of this eighth chapter: "When the apostles which were at Jerusalem heard that Samaria had received the Word of God, they sent unto them Peter, and John: Who, when they were come down, prayed for them, that they might receive the Holy Ghost: (For as yet He was fallen upon none of them: only they were baptized in the name of the Lord Jesus). Then laid they hands on them, and they received the Holy Ghost. And when Simon saw that through laying on of the apostles' hands the Holy Ghost was given, he offered them money, Saying, Give me also this power, that on whomsoever I lay hands, he may receive the Holy Ghost."

As we begin to analyze these verses we see a number of striking things.

1. Although mighty miracles were being constantly manifested, still not one had received the Holy Spirit through Philip's ministry.

2. When Peter and John laid hands on them they received the Holy Spirit.

3. There is no record of any failing to receive the Holy Spirit on whom Peter and John laid hands.

4. They were all new converts, having been saved only a short time.

5. They had been saved and baptized in water (following Peter's formula in Acts 2:38).

6. Simon saw that it was through the laying on of hands that the Holy Spirit was given.

7. There is not the least suggestion that they were taught to tarry for the Holy Spirit, and may we say at this point that teaching people to tarry for that which God has already given as a free gift, only produces doubt and indecision.

The next recorded instance of anyone receiving the Holy Spirit is found in Acts 9:17, "And Ananias went his way, and entered into the house; and putting his hands on him said, Brother Saul, the Lord, even Jesus, that appeared unto thee in the way as thou camest, hath sent me, that thou mightest receive thy sight, and be filled with the Holy Ghost." Now let us see what led up to this happening recorded here. Saul was on his way to Damascus to persecute the Christians. When near the city he was struck down by the power of God, seeing a great light, and hearing the voice of Jesus telling him that he was wrong in persecuting Him. He yielded his heart to God right there, but he was blind when he arose. He was led in this condition into the city, and to the house of Judas, where he sat blind for three days. Then God spoke to a man named Ananias, telling him to go and minister to Saul. Notice, if you will, what Ananias did, and what was the result. What things are most noticeable in this case?

1. Saul was a new convert, saved only three days.

2. Ananias laid his hands on him, and said that he was sent that Saul might receive sight, and be filled with the Holy Spirit.

3. There was no doubt in Ananias' mind that Saul would receive the Holy Spirit.

4. Ananias knew nothing about Saul's spiritual condition other than that he was praying and had seen him (Ananias) in a vision coming to minister to him.

5. There is not a suggestion of tarrying for the Holy Spirit, it being most probable that Saul knew nothing of Him till Ananias came.

6. Saul was an Israelite.

7. Ananias was not an apostle, but an obscure saint, such as you or I.

The next record of people receiving the Holy Spirit is found in Acts 10:44-47. Before this, we have the extended account of Peter's vision of the great sheet let down from Heaven, and its results. He had gone from Joppa to Caesarea, to the house of

Cornelius, where there was gathered a considerable number of Cornelius' kinsmen, and near friends, to hear Peter's message that would tell them how to be saved (Acts 11:14). Then Peter began preaching Jesus to them, and, "While Peter yet spake these words, the Holy Ghost fell on all them which heard the Word. And they of the circumcision which believed were astonished, as many as came with Peter, because that on the Gentiles also was poured out the gift of the Holy Ghost. For they heard them speak with tongues, and magnify God. Then answered Peter, Can any man forbid water, that these should not be baptized, which have received the Holy Ghost as well as we?" Now what do we find here of interest to us?

1. These men were all Gentiles.

2. They were not saved until Peter came. (Acts 11:13-14) "And he showed us how he had seen an angel in his house, which stood and said unto him, Send men to Joppa, and call for Simon, whose surname is Peter; who shall tell thee words, whereby thou and all thy house shall be saved."

3. They received salvation and the Holy Spirit simultaneously.

4. No one laid hands on them.

5. They all received at or near the same time.

6. There were none which failed to receive the Holy Spirit.

7. Speaking with tongues fully convinced Peter's company that these Gentiles had received the Holy Spirit.

8. The Jewish believers were astonished that the Holy Spirit was poured out on Gentiles.

Among the hundreds who have received the Holy Spirit in our meetings we have had many saved and filled with the Spirit all at once. In fact, almost all who have been saved through our ministry in recent months, have received the blessed Comforter before they have left the meeting. We never could forget an incident of this nature which happened quite a number of years ago. We had preached on the receiving of the Holy Spirit, and then had invited any who wished to receive Him, to come and sit on the front row of seats. First a man came, then a young lady came and sat in the second seat from him. As we kept on singing a chorus, waiting for others who might come, the Spirit of God began to move on a young lady in the third row back, next to the aisle on my left. We went down quickly from the platform and laid hands on her, and immediately she began to speak with other tongues. She had only been speaking a few seconds when a young lady, who was sitting in the back of the building, arose and walked up the aisle and took her place on the front row. The moment she was seated we saw that heavenly glow on her face, which indicated that the Spirit was moving upon her, so we laid hands on her at once. Without a moment's delay she burst forth powerfully speaking with other tongues in a clear free language. She had been speaking only a few seconds when she abruptly pulled herself to a stop and said, "I don't understand this." She was shaking so violently, because of holding back the speaking that she could hardly give attention to my explanation of what was happening. I started to explain to her as follows: "Now you are the child of earthly parents, the citizen of an earthly kingdom, living in a world of material things, and you have a natural language which is your means of communication in every contact of life. When you were saved you became the child of a Heavenly Kingdom. You became a spiritual being in a sense you had never been before, and you entered into spiritual relationships which you had never known before and so it is perfectly natural that you should have a divine supernatural language, which is a means of communication with God in the realm of spiritual things." I explained the part about the natural things, and the natural language, and she nodded her head in assent, as she was so full she could scarcely speak. Then I said, "When you were saved—" At this point she interrupted me and said, "Saved! Saved! What do you mean?" I was so amazed at her question that I hardly knew what to say. I supposed she was one of their young people's group, as I was a stranger in that church. When I investigated, I found that she was a rank sinner when she started down that aisle. Her coming was an act of faith; and she was saved as she walked up there, and began speaking with tongues within a few seconds of the time she took her seat. When I explained it all to her, she raised her hands, and began speaking with other tongues, and did not stop for more than two hours. Years later I checked up on this young lady and she was still earnestly serving God. Here was a case such as we have recorded in Acts 10:44-47.

We could tell many experiences where people were saved and received the Holy Spirit all within a few minutes. As I write this I think of what happened in the meeting just last night. Four brothers went into the prayer room to be instructed as to how to be saved. We spoke to them for some time, building faith from the Word, and then knelt down and led them in a prayer of acceptance of Christ. Before they rose from their knees all of them received the Holy Spirit, and were speaking with other tongues as the Spirit gave them utterance.

Now turning to Acts 19:1-7 we have the last recorded case in the New Testament where it speaks of people receiving the Holy Spirit. Paul came, in his travels, to the Gentile city of Ephesus, and there he found some disciples of Apollos, who had only heard the message of John the Baptist (Acts 18:24-28). Paul preached to them salvation through Jesus Christ, and when they heard this, they were baptized in the name of the Lord Jesus. They were not saved men before Paul came, although they were earnest followers of all the light they had. He asked if they had received the Holy Spirit, and they said they knew nothing about the matter. Now after Paul had preached salvation to them, and baptized them, he laid his hands on them and they received the Holy Spirit, speaking with tongues and prophesying. Now, what can we learn from this record?

1. These men were all Gentiles.

2. They were new converts.

3. They received the Holy Spirit when Paul laid his hands on them.

4. They all received without any exception.

5. There is no suggestion of tarrying.

6. They spoke with tongues and prophesied.

Now, after examining all the records concerning the receiving of the Holy Spirit in the early church we may readily draw certain conclusions.

1. There is not a suggestion that the people of the early church were taught to tarry for the Holy Spirit. (The tarrying before, and receiving at Pentecost was all done before there was any

church or dispensation of the Holy Spirit.) If tarrying were God's appointed program for this church age, why didn't the early apostles teach people to tarry in order to receive the Holy Spirit?

2. All who were dealt with received the Holy Spirit as far as recorded, and the Bible is faithful to record failures as well as victories.

3. There was an initial outpouring of the Spirit on Jews at Pentecost, and on Gentiles at the house of Cornelius, where no one laid hands on them.

4. After the initial outpouring of the Spirit on Jews and Gentiles we have no record of any receiving, except as some Spirit-filled person laid hands on them.

5. Apparently everyone does not have the ministry of laying on of hands for the receiving of the Holy Spirit, as none received in Philip's revival at Samaria until Peter and John came down and laid hands on them.

6. Some might contend that only apostles would have the ministry of laying on of hands that people might receive the Holy Spirit, but we should be reminded that Ananias, who laid hands on the great Apostle Paul, when he received the Holy Spirit, was not an apostle, but an obscure saint, who is mentioned only a very few times in the New Testament.

7. Speaking with tongues was sufficient proof to the early disciples that the ones who thus spoke had received the Holy Spirit. (Acts 10:46-47.)

Someone might ask why Peter did not lay hands on the people at Cornelius' house, as he had previously done at Samaria, if that was the plan for the church age. We answer that Peter could not have been induced to lay hands on these Gentiles, since the church in general did not understand that Gentiles were eligible to receive these great blessings which the death and resurrection of Christ had made possible. Notice, the Jewish brethren were astonished when the Holy Spirit fell on Gentiles (Acts 10:45). God had to do a new thing in order to show the Jewish believers that this gospel was for all men who would believe. If anyone cares to take the trouble to go into the back history of the present confirmation service, as carried on in a number of churches, he will find the pattern in the early church. When the present day church official lays hands on the candidate he says, "Receive ye the Holy Ghost." Now, sad to say, in most cases this laying on of hands has become an empty form and nothing supernatural happens, but the pattern they are following was the regular practice in the early church, and the candidate did receive the Holy Spirit and speak with tongues. (Acts 8:17; 9:17; 19:6.)

Chapter IX

REASONS WHY THE HOLY SPIRIT COULD NOT BE GIVEN ON THE BASIS OF OUR PERSONAL HOLINESS

Although it has been very generally taught that the Holy Spirit is given when the seeker has arrived at a high degree of consecration and spirituality; still there is nothing in the New Testament to support such an idea. The fact is that the Holy Spirit was given at Pentecost, following the ascension of Jesus, and He has been here from that day to this, ready to come into any Christian who will open his heart's door and receive Him. The present day question is not, Will God fill this or that Christian with the Holy Spirit? The question is, Will the Christian receive the Holy Spirit whom God has already given? Any Christian, who understands what the Bible teaches, can receive the Holy Spirit at once if he wills to do so, just the same as any one who will, can be saved at once, if he knows what the Bible teaches. It is utterly foolish and illogical, and also it is a libel against the character of God, to say that a man cannot receive the Holy Spirit at once, when God has commanded all Christians to do so—Eph. 5:18. Still, in the face of these facts, we have multiplied thousands of people who have earnestly sought the Holy Spirit for years, and have not yet received Him. Now you may say, "Well, they need not have waited all that time." But they did, and we were not able to instruct them so that they could receive the Holy Spirit, or we would have done so. Now you feel that a minister who could not instruct a man, who wanted to be saved, how to accept Christ, and come to a definite knowledge of salvation, was very poorly prepared for the work to which God had called him. The fact is that every saved person should be able to take his Bible, and lead another person to Christ, and to the definite knowledge that he is a born again child of God.

Then since the Holy Spirit is already given, and to be received by the believer on the same basis as salvation (that is by faith), certainly we should be able to instruct him in the teaching of God's Word, so that he might intelligently receive God's gracious GIFT. We all admit that any saved person would go to be with the Lord if he should die, and yet multitudes of saved people have been told that they were not spiritually prepared to receive the Holy Spirit. How utterly inconsistent is such teaching. Which is the greater experience; standing uncondemned in the presence of God and the glories of Heaven, or receiving the Holy Spirit here on earth? Certainly to enter the glories of Heaven, clothed in the righteousness of Christ, is an incomparably greater experience than to receive the Holy Spirit here, which is one of the means God has given to fully prepare us for Heaven. To put the means above the end is contrary to all logic and sense. Any saved person is ready to receive the Holy Spirit if he knows what the Word teaches.

Now there are many reasons why the Holy Spirit could not be given because of our personal holiness or spirituality, and we herewith give some of them:

1. To begin with, the Word of God always puts the receiving of the Holy Spirit on the basis of grace, a gift of God (Acts 2:37-39; Luke 11:11-13). If you will notice Jesus' promise to pray the Father that He might send you another Comforter is an unconditional promise. He did not say that if people met certain conditions, the Holy Spirit would be sent, but made the simple statement that the Father would send the Comforter, the Holy Ghost, in His name. (John 14:16, 17 & 26.) When the Day of Pentecost came, this promise was fulfilled, and from that day to this He (the Holy Spirit) has been here. It is unscriptural and unbelieving to pray God to send Him, when He is already here.

In Acts 2:38 and 39 we read, "Repent, and be baptized every one of you in the name of Jesus Christ for the remission of sins, and ye shall receive the gift of the Holy Ghost. For the promise is unto you, and to your children, and to all that are afar off, even as many as the Lord our God shall call." Let us notice two words in verse 38 carefully. The first important word is GIFT. God here speaks of the Holy Spirit as a gift. If we worked for it or deserved it, then it would not be a gift, but would be wages or a reward for merit (Rom. 4:4). The only righteousness we have, or can have, that makes us eligible to receive the Holy Spirit is the imputed righteousness of Christ which is credited to us because of our faith in His sacrifice for us.

Now let us look at the other important word, which is RECEIVE. The word receive applies to an act of the one who gets something, and not to an act of the giver. God has already given the Spirit, and it is now the man's move. He can receive the Spirit if he wills to do so, if he has been correctly taught what the Bible teaches on this subject. We have proved this last statement in hundreds of cases recently, and usually all receive the Spirit who are scripturally dealt with.

Again Luke 11:13 makes it plain that the Holy Spirit is given on the basis of gift, and not of works. "If ye then, being evil, know how to give good gifts unto your children: how much more shall your heavenly Father give the Holy Spirit to them that ask Him?"

Then there are three most important verses in the third chapter of Galatians which bear upon this subject. Paul says, "This only would I learn of you, Received ye the Spirit by the works of the law, or by the hearing of faith?" (verse 2) Here he plainly shows that the Spirit is received by faith and not by obedience to the law. Then verse five gives us a new and revolutionary thought. "He therefore that ministereth to you the Spirit, and worketh miracles among you, doeth he it by the works of the law, or by the hearing of faith?" It points out that the Spirit was ministered to believers by other believers and that it was a matter of faith on the part of the one who ministered the Spirit to others. Isn't that exactly what Ananias did to Paul (Acts 9:17), and did not Peter and John minister the Spirit to that group of believers at Samaria? Read the account in Acts 8, and notice how it says that Simon saw that by the laying on of the Apostles' hands the Holy Spirit was given. They believed, when they laid hands on them, and they saw the candidates receive the Holy Spirit.

Also Galatians 3:13 and 14 declares that we receive the promise of the Spirit by faith and not by works. This one reason alone, with the Scriptures given, should be enough to convince any logical, thinking person that the Holy Spirit is not given on the basis of good works and our personal holiness; but in the face of these facts, we meet people constantly who have not received the Holy Spirit, and they will tell you that they have never felt they were good enough to receive Him.

They may not have been directly taught this idea, but they certainly have been allowed to continue believing it. Regardless of where they got the idea, the result is the same. They do not receive the Holy Spirit as long as they believe they are not yet holy enough, and it cannot be denied that most people who have not received, believe that spiritual lack is the thing which has hindered them from receiving Him. We find that most of these people will receive the Holy Spirit at once when shown what the Bible really teaches.

2. Everyone who knows anything about God, knows that absolute justice must be one of His primary characteristics. He must be entirely fair and no respecter of persons if He is God. (Acts 10:34.) Now if the Holy Spirit were given on the basis of our having arrived at a certain degree of consecration and victory over sinful and binding habits, then it would be God's duty to make every one arrive at exactly the same degree of holiness and consecration before He would fill him with the Spirit. If he did not do so, He would be unjust and would be showing favoritism. This we know, God will not and cannot do. If, however, we look at the recorded cases in the Book of Acts, where people received the Holy Spirit, we will see that in four out of five cases, whole groups of people received the Holy Spirit at the same time. Now it is unreasonable to suppose, and unthinkable to a logical mind, that the people in these various groups had all arrived at the same spiritual level at the same time. Where could we find even two people at exactly the same level of spirituality at the same time, much less whole groups of them? (See Acts 2:4; 8:17; 10:44-48; 19:1-7.) Either God is unjust or the Holy Spirit is not given on the basis of our holiness and consecration. Again we repeat the statement that the imputed righteousness of Christ is the only righteousness we have, which gives us the least particle of standing in the sight of God, making us worthy to receive any

of His benefits. They are given on the basis of grace and grace alone.

3. Another proof of our statement that the Holy Spirit is not given on the basis of our spirituality is as follows: If spiritual lack were the hindering factor which keeps the seeker from receiving the Holy Spirit, then it would be the duty of a just and loving God to show the seeker what it is that is keeping him from receiving the promise. Still thousands of earnest seekers have searched their hearts for years and years, and have asked God to show them where their lack was, and yet you will never find one person who is earnestly seeking the Holy Spirit, who knows what is hindering him from receiving. Would you punish a child of yours and at the same refuse to tell the child why you were punishing him? Most certainly not; and still the teaching that the Holy Spirit is given on the basis of our holiness accuses God of doing that very thing, for surely it is punishment to the hungry seeker to be unable to receive. What an insult to God! The writer has questioned many seekers on this point and every one will say he has done every thing he can think of to prepare himself, and that he does not know what is hindering him. In fact he will usually tell you that he has tried everything that anyone has suggested to him, but all to no avail. However, because of his earnestness, he goes on seeking, always hoping that he will eventually find his way through the fog that clouds the whole affair. If this kind of situation were according to God's plan, why do not we have some record of it in the Bible? There is not a record where any failed to receive the Holy Suirit who were dealt with. Let us stop accusing God of treating His children worse than we would treat ours, and let us believe His Word, "Ye shall RECEIVE the GIFT of the Holy Ghost." The factor which really hinders people from receiving is dealt with in another chapter of this book.

4. Again, if the Holy Spirit were given on the basis of our having reached a certain spiritual standard, then it would be the duty of a just and loving God to clearly lay out in His Word what the candidate would have to do to reach the required standard. We find, however, on searching the Word that there is no set of standards which we are told we will have to meet in

order to be filled with the Holy Spirit. The only thing we are told
to do in order to receive the Holy Spirit is found in Acts 2:38,
"Repent and be baptized." Repentance, as used here, involves
believing in the crucified and risen Christ, which brings us into
salvation. Now it is God's order that salvation should come first,
then water baptism, and next the receiving of the Holy Spirit,
but in two of five cases recorded in the Book of Acts the people
received the Holy Spirit before water baptism. (Acts 9:17-18; Acts
10:44-48.) We notice in Acts 19:1-6 how Paul follows the order
that Peter gave in Acts 2:37-39, and this evidently is God's plan,
but we must admit that both in the Bible record and in our
experience there are those who receive the Holy Spirit before
being baptized in water.

Some might object that the Word says He will give the Holy
Spirit to those that obey Him. (Acts 5:22) That obedience could
not cover more than the obedience to the commands spoken of
as necessary to the receiving of the Holy Spirit, which we have
just discussed. If it implied general obedience to all God's commands then no one could ever receive, because no one ever
perfectly obeyed the Lord's commands. That is the reason that
no one could ever be justified by keeping the law. God's holiness
demands absolute perfection and none of us is perfect. Again we
repeat, the only righteousness we have which gives us any standing with God is the imputed righteousness of Christ which is
credited to our account, the righteousness which is by faith in
Jesus Christ.

Let us here remind the reader that our right to receive the
Holy Spirit is just another manifestation of the great love and
matchless grace of our risen Savior. You will never be worthy
to receive on the basis of your own righteousness, so come in the
merits of our glorious Lord.

5. We submit one more proof that the Holy Spirit is given on
the basis of grace and not of merit. We speak of the present day
experience in our Full Gospel churches throughout the land.
Every minister who has given any thought and attention to this
matter knows that the most godly, dependable, and prayerful
people are very often the last ones to receive the Holy Spirit,
while the rather unstable, and undependable and erratic type

of people will usually receive almost at once. Very often the ones who fall into the ranks of those classified as "chronic" seekers are among the very best and most solid Christians in the church. Why do not they receive? is the question. If holiness was the condition, they should be the first to receive, but they are not. Now let us see why they fail to receive as soon as the others. Here is the answer. They have been taught, or at least allowed to believe, that their personal holiness is the determining factor. Now their very conscientiousness is the thing that has hindered them. They are always feeling that they are not holy enough yet, and Satan encourages them in that belief. They, because of their godly character, want to be very sure that they do not do something "in the flesh" as they say, which is supposed to be of the Spirit. The result is that they constantly hold back when the Spirit moves upon them, and do not receive.

On the other hand the reckless, unstable type of people do not stop to question their holiness and just throw themselves with abandon upon the Lord and receive at once. This condition has been a great source of stumbling to many, and has caused much confusion among God's people. The matter of what actually happens when a person receives the Holy Spirit and speaks with other tongues is taken up more fully in another chapter.

After facing all these facts honestly we surely can come to no other conclusion than that the Holy Spirit is received on the basis of grace and grace alone.

Chapter X

TRAGEDIES RESULTING FROM THE TEACHING THAT THE HOLY SPIRIT IS GIVEN ON THE BASIS OF OUR PERSONAL HOLINESS AND CONSECRATION

All who have had any considerable contact with those present day Christian bodies which teach that the receiving of the Holy Spirit will be accompanied by the supernatural sign of speaking with other tongues, know that there has been a tragic amount of backsliding, shallow Christian living, and splits and divisions among them. Does this mean that they are wrong in teaching that the supernatural signs and powers, which characterized the early church, are to be expected in the churches of Jesus Christ today? Most assuredly not. Does it mean that the teaching of these things is the cause of their failures to be what Christ intended His church to be? Our answer certainly must be NO.

We are living in the same dispensation in which Peter and Paul lived; the dispensation of the Holy Spirit, and if there is anything which should characterize the church of our Lord in this dispensation, it is the supernatural signs and powers which were everywhere apparent in the early beginnings. Scripture is full of the teachings that the Christian church should be a miracle working institution from beginning to end, divinely empowered by the blessed Holy Spirit. (Mark 16:16-20; John 14:12; Heb. 2:4; Isa. 8:18.) Then where lies the difficulty? Why the discrepancies which are all too apparent? Must we give up in despair and say these things cannot be correct? By no means. If we will honestly face facts, and act in line with the blessed Word of God, we can go sweeping on to glorious victory, fulfilling the mission God has for us in these last days of this Holy Spirit dispensation, performing miracles in the power of the Holy Spirit.

Now the trouble lies, not in the fact that we have taught that Christians should receive the Holy Spirit with the supernatural signs following, but in the basis upon which we have taught that the Holy Spirit and His powers should be received. It has been almost universally taught that the Holy Spirit and His gifts are received on basis of human merit, instead of on the basis of Grace, as the Bible so plainly teaches; and many tragic results have followed. We propose, on the following pages, to point out some of these tragedies which have so greatly hindered the usefulness of this blessed Spirit-filled movement.

The Apostle Paul pointed out the fact that the church at Corinth "came behind in no gift," and still it needed a great deal of corrective instruction in order to be what the church of Christ should be, and surely our present day Spirit-filled movement could be helped by the same means.

1. The first tragedy we wish to speak of is this. As long as people believe that the Holy Spirit is given on the basis of human merit (and most of them do, because of teaching or tradition) it gives Satan a lever with which to hold earnest seekers from receiving Him. He (Satan) can find in the best of people plenty of things which are not perfect, and he is ever ready to point out these, telling the seekers for the Holy Spirit that they are not yet holy enough. Now the most godly and consecrated people are the ones who are most affected by this trick of the enemy of their souls. They are very anxious to meet every requirement that God has made, so that they go on for years, struggling to become holy enough to receive the Holy Spirit. Since they believe that the receiving is on the basis of their personal holiness, they play right into the hands of Satan, and he keeps them in a state of doubt and discouragement through the years they spend waiting. If they could have been correctly taught, and had known the truth, that the Holy Spirit is given as a free gift of God's grace, they might have spent those years in powerful Spirit-filled service for God. Instead of looking at their own failures and being depressed and defeated by them, they would have taken blessed victory over them in the power of the Holy Spirit.

2. Another tragedy which has resulted from this unscriptural teaching is that when the seeker for the Holy Spirit does receive Him, and speaks with tongues supernaturally, he very often

assumes that his character is fully pleasing to God. His reasoning is as follows: If the Holy Spirit is given on the basis of my having arrived at a high degree of consecration and holiness, then, I must have arrived at that level of spirituality which is fully pleasing to God. He is very often proud, arrogant and unteachable, because he feels that he has arrived at the pinnacle of Christian experience. Now where is he to go? Many times he becomes slack and careless in his Christian life and is less useful after he received the Holy Spirit than he was before. He must look behind him to see the apex of his Christian experience, and that is tragic in any one's life. Surely our Christian life should be a steady growth, ever ascending to greater heights of faith, holiness and Christlikeness as the years go by. The person who feels he has passed the greatest experience of his Christian life cannot possibly have the correct viewpoint. He does not realize that the receiving of the Holy Spirit is on the basis of grace, and therefore no credit is due him whatever. He does not see that the Holy Spirit was given so that we might receive Him, and thus be led by Him into all truth. He does not know that the Holy Spirit was given, not because we are holy, but in order that by His help, we might grow to be more Christlike. The actual fact is that the individual has no more character immediately after he has received the Holy Spirit than he had before, but he has a source of help and power to build Christian character which cannot be over estimated. In closing this thought let us say that a very large part of those who believe that they received the Holy Spirit because of their Christian character do not go on to develop in Christlikeness, as God intended them to do. Shall we, as Spirit-filled people, allow this sad tragedy to be constantly re-enacted in the lives of others, when it might be largely prevented by correct Scriptural teaching?

✓ 3. One of the saddest results of this unscriptural teaching is this: it casts a reflection on the character of those who do not receive the Holy Spirit, and very often they are among the most spiritual and godly people in the church. The reasoning of those who have received the Holy Spirit is something like this: "Now since the Holy Spirit is given because of our holiness, and since Sister So-and-so does not receive Him, it must be true that there

is sin in her life. So far as we can see she is an ideal Christian.
She is always at prayer meeting, and every other meeting of the
church. She is always ready to sit up with the sick and care for
the needy. No, we can see very few faults in her, and much to
indicate holiness, but there just must be hidden sin somewhere or
God would give her the Holy Spirit." (Let us remind the reader
at this point that God has already given the Holy Spirit, and He
can be received at once by any Christian who has correct Scriptural teaching. It is not a question of God's willingness to give,
but of the seeker's lack of knowledge of what the Spirit is trying
to get him to do.) Let us return now to our sister who fails to
receive the Holy Spirit. Since the others feel that there must be
hidden sin in her life, it is almost sure, sooner or later, that she
will hear what is being said about her. She knows that what they
have said is not true, but she has no way of proving it to them.
She is heart-broken, for she knows she is doing her utmost, by
God's help, to live a holy life. Often she knows that she is living
closer to the Lord than those who are finding fault with her, and
yet, they have received the Holy Spirit and she has not. She is
puzzled and distressed by the situation, and very often gives
up seeking altogether. Her faith has been given a terrific blow,
since she has not received what God's Word promises her. In a
great many Full Gospel assemblies there are some who are in
this sad condition. They cannot be induced to seek the Holy
Spirit any more, as they have been disappointed so often that
they feel it is no use. We have found, however, that most of these
will receive when they are shown that we receive Him on the
basis of grace and not of works.

4. This teaching reduces the possibility of leading those who
have received the Holy Spirit on to be fully developed Christians.
Since they have arrived, according to their ideas, at a high point
of spirituality, and since they have received the Holy Spirit,
they feel that they need no one to teach them. Really, what is
there for them to learn? Haven't they arrived at the desired
goal? Too often this is their attitude. Now we are not suggesting
that even a large per cent take this position, but the teaching that
we receive the Holy Spirit on the basis of our holiness does leave
the door open for the receiver to feel this way. Why not teach

him, as the Bible does, that he has done nothing meritorious at all in receiving the Holy Spirit, but that the gift is just another proof of the limitless grace of God? With that idea in mind he will realize that he has just entered the door of greater usefulness, and that his possibilities for growing in grace and doing God's work are greatly increased.

5. This teaching puts us in a place where we must declare that many who apparently received the Holy Spirit, and spoke with other tongues, did not receive the real thing, but that they had a spurious experience. According to the prevalent conception, the receiving of the Holy Spirit is proof of real Christian character. In fact, it must be true if He is received on the basis of human merit. Now our experience has shown us that a great host of people have received the Holy Spirit and spoken with other tongues, but instead of manifesting the character of holiness of life which we thought they should, they have lived very careless and shallow lives, often conducting themselves in a way which any Christian knows is displeasing to God. Now what are we going to do about it? If we hold to our theories, we will be forced to say they must not have gotten the real Holy Spirit. A very godly young minister said to the writer that he discounted the experience of at least seventy-five per cent of those who were supposed to have received the Holy Spirit. He claimed that their experiences were not genuine because they subsequently failed to measure up in their Christian development to the standard he had set for Spirit-filled people. We have no scriptural ground for taking such a position. In the Bible records they declared, without hesitation, that the people who spoke with other tongues had received the Holy Spirit. If Peter had followed this brother's theory he would have said, at the house of Cornelius (Acts 10:44-48), "Now these people have all spoken with tongues, but I must reserve judgment for six months or so before I can confidently state that they have received the Holy Spirit. I want to see how they live first." What he did do was to say at once, "These have received the Holy Ghost as well as we." We do not suppose that all of that group developed as Peter would have liked to see them develop; but he recognized the principle that they were free moral agents, or free to make their own decisions,

and that, even though they had received the Holy Spirit, they were not forced to walk in the way He would subsequently lead them. Sad, but true, many do not allow the Holy Spirit to have full control in their lives, even though He is abiding in them. They only yield partially to Him in His endeavor to lead them God's way, and thus they fail to develop as they should.

Now we have yet to find in the Word of God any suggestion that the Christian may receive a false experience when seeking for the Holy Spirit. The fact is that all the Scriptures point in just the opposite direction. (Read Luke 11:11-13.) If the Christian cannot come to God in confidence that he will receive the real Holy Spirit when he asks according to the Word, then, we ask, what can he be sure of? We believe that all the suggestions concerning the possibility of receiving false or worthless experiences, have done nothing but build doubts and fears in the minds of people until a great number of them have been seriously hindered in their forward march with God. Why build doubts and fears, when the pure Word of God will build faith and confidence, and lead people on to be more like Christ? Surely that is the goal toward which we all should have our faces set with God-given determination.

6. Since it has been the general teaching and conception that the receiving of the Holy Spirit and spiritual gifts is on the basis of our spirituality, therefore the possession of the Holy Spirit and spiritual gifts would necessarily be a proof of holiness. Now many, because of this mis-conception, take the stand that their lives must be right and pleasing to God because they still speak with tongues, when they are living very unholy lives. They do not seem to realize that God gives His gifts, and then leaves it up to us as to whether we use them for His glory or not. They fail to realize that genuine spiritual gifts may be misused. A careful study of First Corinthians will reveal that they had all the spiritual gifts in their church, but still they were living in a way that was far from pleasing to God. In I Corinthians 13 the Apostle Paul never once suggests that the gifts mentioned were not genuine, but he very clearly points out that if the one who manifested them was not motivated by love, he (not the gift) was nothing, and it profited him nothing. Surely it is made plain

here that genuine gifts might be manifested by those whose lives were not right. Whenever we take the position that manifesting of spiritual gifts is a proof of a holy life, we are preparing, almost certainly, for disastrous results. A number of places in the Bible we find ungodly men manifesting genuine spiritual gifts; Saul prophesied when seeking the life of righteous David (I Sam. 19:20-24). Read the story of Balaam in Numbers, chapters 22, 23, 24 and 25. Surely Balaam was not right, and still some of the most wonderful prophecies in the Bible concerning Israel came out of his mouth. In John 11:49-52 we find Caiaphas prophesying concerning Jesus' death for our sins, and still he was plotting right then to help murder Him. The possession of spiritual gifts lays on us an increased responsibility to live a holy life, but the fact that we have these gifts is no proof at all that we are meeting our responsibility. At the day of accounting it will surely go badly with those who have been gifted with spiritual gifts and still have failed to live holy lives. Let no misguided soul judge his spirituality to be at a high level just because he speaks with tongues. The Word says, "By their fruits ye shall know them" (Matt. 7:20; Gal. 5:22-23), and not by their gifts. No gift can ever be proof of character, since gifts are received in a moment of time, while the fruit of the Spirit, which makes up our true character, is slowly developed in the life of the believer.

7. This mistaken idea that the Holy Spirit is given on the basis of our holiness keeps many from going on to speak with tongues in their private prayer life. Surely the Word makes it very clear that Spirit-filled people should follow this practice regularly. (We refer the reader to the chapter dealing with this point.) We have found a great number of people who were afraid to go ahead and speak with other tongues because they felt they were not holy enough. They have allowed Satan to make them believe that if they spoke with tongues when they were imperfect they would be sinning against the Holy Spirit, and thus they have been shut out from using one of the means God has given us for spiritual upbuilding. "He that speaketh in an unknown tongue edifieth himself." (See I Cor. 14:4; also verses 2, and 14-18.) These people are conscientious, who fear they will displease God, and are just the opposite of those who claim holiness

simply because they speak with tongues. Usually when these people have been shown the truth that the speaking with tongues is a God-given means of edification and spiritual victory, they have, with a little encouragement, begun to speak with tongues again, and we have many testimonies of those whose private prayer life has been completely revolutionized by seeing the truth and acting in accordance with it.

8. Another tragedy we wish to mention resulting from the teaching that the Holy Spirit is given on the basis of our personal holiness, and consecration, is that a great number of the best people we might have reached with this blessed message concerning the Spirit-filled life, have been permanently shut out from its blessings, by what they have seen and heard. They have been led to believe that the receiving of the Spirit was proof of a godly, consecrated life, but when they saw people who had received the Holy Spirit, and spoken with other tongues, live in a way which most certainly did not demonstrate a high type of morality, and godliness, they were confused completely, and decided that they did not care to receive the Spirit. Their reasoning is something like this, "Now I want to be a victorious, overcoming Christian, and I want all God has for me, but if the receiving of the Holy Spirit, with the evidence of speaking with other tongues, has the effect on people that I have observed in some cases I do not believe I want this experience." Remember, reader, that Satan is always ready to point out the failures, and cover up the successes of Christians. Almost always the unsaved man's attention is fixed on the poorest examples in the church, and on the basis of these observations, he judges the whole organization. He often says that they are all a bunch of hypocrites, completely ignoring the great multitude of earnest godly Christians, which make up a large part of the church. He doesn't realize that a new Christian is just a babe in Christ, and cannot be expected to demonstrate that maturity of Christian development, which is seen in those who have gone on to grow spiritually over a long period. Now, since Satan fights anything which will help God's people to greater victory, he fights the receiving of the Holy Spirit, and points out to the prospective seekers the failures among Spirit-filled people. If these people were made to understand that the

receiving of the Holy Spirit is on the basis of grace instead of works, and that the receiving of the Spirit is no proof whatever of Christian character, they would not be so likely to be thrown into confusion by seeing Spirit-filled people live shallow, careless Christian lives.

Many who have been held back from receiving the Spirit, would enter in and receive Him, if they understood these principles. The group that has thus been shut out is of no insignificant size. It includes tens of thousands of solid intelligent people all over the land.

Now we are not, in any way, excusing the shallow careless living of these who have been the cause of hindrance. Surely the receiving of the Holy Spirit gives the individual greater power to live a godly life, and it lays on him a greater responsibility to do so, but it is no proof at all that he WILL do so. We are all free moral agents, but many, sad to say, do not use the means God has put at their disposal to build Christian character. We often hear people ask the question, "Did not Jesus say that people would receive power after receiving the Holy Spirit? Then why do we see so many powerless, ineffective Christians, who have received the Spirit?" Our answer again is that people are free to make their own choices, and are not compelled to use the power God has given them. Imagine a situation like this. Here is a skillful carpenter, who has a building lot, a set of plans for the building, and all the materials necessary to build the house according to the plans, but he has no tools of any kind. With this set-up he is helpless to build the building, but if you would bring him a tool chest full of all the good tools he needs, at once he would be given power to build the house, but remember, he might sit down on top of the tool chest and fold his hands. It lies within his power to work or remain idle, and the possession of tools constitutes no guarantee that he will use them. So it is with the man who has received the Holy Spirit. He has power divinely given of God, but he, like the carpenter, may sit down and fold his hands.

9. Another tragic thing which has happened among us because of the teaching that the Holy Spirit is received on the basis of our Christian character is that many ministers have become

discouraged, and are either backslidden entirely, or are no longer preaching the blessed truth that Christians should receive the Holy Spirit today, the same as in the days of the apostles. This is a natural result of this unscriptural teaching. Having been led to believe that Christians would demonstrate a high type of Christian life, after receiving the Holy Spirit, and speaking supernaturally with other tongues, they have been swept off their feet entirely when they saw many, who spoke with other tongues, fail to go on and live as Christians ought to do. Many churches, of those denominations which do not teach this blessed truth, have great numbers in their ranks who have received the Holy Spirit, and at one time spoke with other tongues. They are there because they became discouraged by seeing people fail to live as they should after receiving the Holy Spirit.

If these ministers, who no longer teach this blessed truth, had been taught that the Holy Spirit was received on the basis of grace, and grace alone, they would have realized that the receiving of the Holy Spirit is no proof whatever of Christian character, and therefore would not have been discouraged when they saw Spirit-filled Christians fail. We are just as much free moral agents after we have received the Holy Spirit as we were before, and the real test of consecration and obedience comes after we have received Him. If we had talked as much about the walk of obedience to the leading of the Spirit after we have received Him, as we have talked about the initial receiving of the Spirit, we would have much more in the way of holy living among our Full Gospel people.

Now these people who failed to measure up to the standards Christians should meet, have not failed because they received the Holy Spirit. They have failed because of other factors in their teaching, and much of the failure and backsliding came because of their mistaken belief that they have a character which is fully pleasing to God, or He would not have filled them with the Holy Spirit.

We have mentioned before that God does not give the Holy Spirit to people today as the terms, which we have used, would suggest. God GAVE the Holy Spirit on the Day of Pentecost, and from that day on, it has been a matter of the man receiving the

Holy Spirit, and not of God giving Him. On the Day of Pentecost God's part in this matter was finished. Now we are dealing with the Holy Spirit, the representative of the Godhead in this dispensation, and He is ready to come in to the body of any Christian who will believe and receive Him. He does not come in because we have arrived at a high state of spiritual development and consecration, but He comes in to cause us, by His help and guidance, to become conformed to the image of Christ. If our ministers had understood this truth, we would have many preaching this blessed message concerning the receiving of the Holy Spirit who have long since ceased to proclaim it.

10. One of the most tragic results of all that has followed the unscriptural teaching, or belief, that the Holy Spirit will be given when we get consecrated, or holy enough, is this: a great many earnest, sincere Christians, after struggling a long time to receive the Holy Spirit without success, have been led, in their discouragement, to believe, that they are not even saved. This plunges them into greater distress, and eventually they give up living a Christian life altogether. It is quite natural that this result should follow such an idea, if the person is a logical thinker. Then let us remember also that Satan is the accuser of the brethren, and he is ever ready to use subtle means to deceive God's children, and discourage them.

Shall we do a little reasoning here, and see where it leads us? If I am a child of God, then I am eligible to receive the Holy Spirit. Acts 2:38-39 reads, "Then Peter said unto them, Repent, and be baptized every one of you in the name of Jesus Christ for the remission of sins, and ye shall receive the gift of the Holy Ghost. For the promise is unto you, and to your children, and to all that are afar off, even as many as the Lord our God shall call." The Word says He was given as a gracious gift, and is to be received by faith and not by works. Let us read Gal. 3:2 and 5: "This only would I learn of you, Received ye the Spirit by the works of the law, or by the hearing of faith?" and "He therefore that ministereth to you the Spirit, and worketh miracles among you, doeth he it by the works of the law, or by the hearing of faith?" I try and try to receive Him, and fail to do so, and Satan comes in at this point and says: "See, you are not eligible to receive the Spirit, or you would have received Him. The fact is you are not even saved; you just thought you were.'" This throws the person into confusion, at is sounds logical, and he does not know how to refute it, as long as he clings to the belief that the Spirit will be given when he becomes eligible. He knows that he wants with all his heart to be what God wants him to be, but, very often, he does not know how to defend himself against this sly attack of the enemy. If he isn't saved, as Satan has suggested, then he doesn't know what to do, because he has done all that he knows to do to be saved. A cloud of depression begins to settle over him, and soon he feels that it is no use trying to be a Christian, and so he gives up completely.

You may say this is far fetched; well, be that as it may, we constantly have such discouraged people come to us with their sad story. They sit with tears running down their cheeks, and ask us if it is possible that they are not saved. Almost invariably the pastors of these people tell us that they are among the finest, most steady, people they have. So far as I can remember, every one of these people has joyfully received the Holy Spirit when shown that He is to be received as a gracious gift from a loving Father. They have blossomed out into sturdy, victorious Christians, living in the sunshine of God's love, having come completely out from under the cloud that Satan had put over their lives.

11. The last point we wish to mention in this chapter is that this wrong concept, as to the basis upon which the Holy Spirit is received, makes the receiving an end in itself, instead of a means to an end. Surely there can be no correct objective for the Christian life other than to be fully like Jesus. If we have no higher purpose than just getting eternal life, we certainly have missed the main point, and that is that we should live a life which fully honors Him, who loved us and gave Himself for us. In no way can we so fully honor Him as to be like Him. Now it is readily seen that being like Him entails the building of Christian character. That is the end we are seeking. If we believe, as many do, that the receiving of the Spirit is the result of arriving at a high degree of spirituality, then the receiving becomes to us an end in itself; for truly the building of Christian character is an end to be sought. What chance is there for much

development for the person who believes he has arrived at an end? How we wish that all might realize that the receiving of the Holy Spirit just equips us to begin a life of greater usefulness to God.

With all these tragic things resulting from this mistaken conception as to the basis upon which the blessed Holy Spirit is received, surely we should do all that is in our power to correct this error, and help both those who have, and those who have not received Him, knowing that the closer we adhere to the Word of God, the more we will be blessed of Him, and honor His great name.

Chapter XI

DEALING WITH THOSE WHO WISH TO RECEIVE THE HOLY SPIRIT

To begin with the Holy Spirit is received by faith, exactly the same as salvation is received (Gal. 3:2, 5, 13 & 14). Now faith is built up in the candidate by correct instructions which make clear to his mind what the Word of God teaches (Rom. 10:17). Faith in anything is based on our knowledge concerning it. For instance, faith that certain mining stocks will bring rich profits comes from what we have been taught about the mines in question, either by observation, our general knowledge of the area where the mines are located, or printed literature and testimony of those interested. Now the Bible tells us that faith concerning eternal things comes through hearing the Word of God. In other words, we find what God's Word teaches concerning a certain matter, and then we can go forward with confidence.

You believe, what you believe about world political and economic conditions, because of what you have been taught by the newspapers, the radio, and all other means of spreading knowledge concerning these things. Now often the things we believe are not true, because we have been wrongly instructed; but when we are taught faithfully what God's Word teaches, we know we will not go wrong in spiritual understanding. His Word is true.

We buy the mining stock because we have faith in the mines. Faith moves us to action. When a person is a candidate to receive the Holy Spirit we should be able to instruct him in what the Bible teaches so clearly and simply that faith can take hold, and he can receive the Holy Spirit at once. To illustrate what wrong teaching will do we cite the following example: Here is a young man who is unsaved, and living with his family who are all saved people. He has come to the place where he sees his need of salvation, and sincerely wants to be saved, but his family has shut the door of salvation in his face. He is bound by the cigarette habit, and they have told him that he never can be saved until he quits his cigarettes. Now carefully analyze this situation. He has confidence in his family, as they live godly lives. He believes what they tell him. Since he believes that he cannot be saved while still using cigarettes, it actually becomes true that he cannot be saved as long as he believes this. Since salvation comes as a result of his believing that the blood of Jesus is a complete, and all sufficient, remedy for his sins, and since he believes he cannot be saved while smoking cigarettes, therefore he cannot be saved, because it is impossible for anyone to believe two contradictory things at the same time. He cannot believe he is saved because he still has the smoking habit, and he cannot stop smoking because he is not saved. The only way to help that man is to get him to see that he can be saved just as he is, with all his vile habits, and then God will clean him up, and deliver him from them. The old hymn, "Just as I am without plea, but that Thy blood was shed for me," brings out this glorious truth. However, multitudes of well meaning Christians, thinking they are holding up holy standards, have shut the door of salvation to many other hungry hearts.

Now wrong teaching concerning the receiving of the Holy Spirit has done the same thing. Multitudes of saved people are longing to be filled with the Spirit, but always believing that they are not yet good enough. We constantly meet those who have sought for years, but have allowed Satan to keep them feeling that they are not yet holy enough. Of course they cannot receive the Holy Spirit with this attitude. Let's face facts honestly. We who have already received are largely to blame for their having such ideas. The Holy Spirit is a GIFT of God's grace, and anyone who is saved is ready to receive the Holy Spirit if he only knows it. We should point out to them that God has already given the Holy Spirit, and that it is up to them to receive that which has already been given. It is not now a proposition of God doing something. He has already done His part. It is a matter of the man doing something. Acts 2:38 and 39 shows this very clearly. It says "Ye shall RECEIVE the gift of the Holy Ghost." The word "receive" applies to an act of the one who gets something, not to an act of the giver. This word "receive" might just as readily be translated "take" and do no injury to the meaning of the original Greek. We should point out to the man, that since speaking with other tongues is the initial outward evidence of the Holy Spirit's coming in, therefore he should expect to speak with other tongues, and set the stage for that to happen. Faith prepares everything for the coming of the desired result. Since it is impossible to speak two languages at once, he should be told to cast aside all thought of speaking his own words so that the Spirit might be free to move upon his lips to form supernatural words. That is faith. It is not demonstrating faith to start off praising God with my own words, and at the same time saying I am expecting supernatural words. (The principles of speaking with other tongues has been discussed in another chapter.) We have yet to find in the Scripture any thing that would warrant our telling the candidate to lift up his hands and praise the Lord, as is so often done by zealous workers. This hinders instead of helps, as has been clearly shown in another place.

How often we have seen an earnest seeker at the altar, desiring to be filled with all the fullness of the Holy Spirit, being hindered by those trying to help him. Many have told the writer that just when they had gotten quiet before the Lord, to the point where the Spirit began to move upon them, so-called helpers came around and so confused them that they gave up in despair. One said to the seeker, "Now hold on, brother." Another just as earnestly entreated, "Now let go, brother, the Holy Spirit is coming in." From another comes the instruction, "Praise the Lord, brother, praise the Lord, you are just about there," while still another shouts, "Now, brother, just yield. That is all you have to do." By this time the Spirit is moving upon the man so powerfully that he is no longer able to speak his own words clearly, and still some sincere, but ignorant, brother or sister will say, "Now brother, are you sure you have consecrated everything?" With all of these helpers, giving their various directions, how can we expect the poor candidate to get his mind settled on anything? Usually he doesn't; but in discouragement finally gets up and goes home wondering why he did not "get through" as is often said. He has every reason to believe that all of his instructors are earnestly trying to help him. He knows that they are good people, and since they have already received the Holy Spirit, it usually does not enter his mind that they are wrong in the methods they are using to try to help him. If they are right then he figures the trouble must be with himself. Where has he failed? Why doesn't God reveal to him what the trouble is? After searching his heart and going over the situation, a great many times, over a period of months or years, and failing to find the answer, he finally gives up in despair, and decides the Holy Spirit just isn't for him.

The Full Gospel movement has today in its ranks literally thousands of such people over the world. You meet them everywhere you go, if you make any inquiry along this line. They will no longer seek the Holy Spirit because they have been disappointed so many times, that faith can no longer rise. What a tragedy that godly, consecrated people have the door to greater blessing and usefulness shut in their faces, by wrong methods being used to try to help them.

Usually when seekers fail to receive the Holy Spirit, and speak with other tongues, it is considered by the others in the church, which have received the Holy Spirit, that there is something wrong spiritually, or there is hidden sin which only God knows about. Thus a reflection is often cast on the character of the man who actually is more godly, and has more real Christian character, than the ones who think there is something wrong with him. It can be most easily proved that it is not a spiritual lack, which hinders earnest seekers from receiving the Holy Spirit. All one has to do to find out is to ask the seeker if he knows what is hindering him. In asking this question of a large number the writer has never yet found one who knew what was hindering him. They will say, "I have done everything I know to do, and have asked God to show me what the trouble is, and He has shown me nothing." Now if the man were not telling the truth, and God had showed him something which hindered, he would do one of two things; he would either put away the thing he knew was hindering, or he would stop seeking the Holy Spirit. Any one who has any ability to reason can see this would evidently follow.

Now let us think of another angle of this thing. If God refused to reveal to the man what was wrong, and still refused to fill him with the Holy Spirit, He would be worse than the man who would punish a child and still refuse to tell the child why he was being punished. No, our God does not follow that kind of unjust and wicked practices. The trouble is not with God, nor with the spiritual life of the seeker. It is the wrong instruction which he has been given that is hindering him. God longs to see him filled with the Spirit (Luke 11:13), but He cannot do the part which is the man's part, otherwise He would be violating the principle of free moral agency. Note: the man's part is to do the speaking. (See chapter on Speaking with Tongues.)

Recently a fine godly young man who received the Holy Spirit so simply, and beautifully, when shown what the Bible teaches, told us that for fourteen years he had been waiting for the Spirit to speak through him. As soon as he understood that it was the man's part to do the speaking, (Acts 2:4 Weymouth) he immediately entered in by faith and soon was glorifying God in a supernatural language. The Spirit had been moving on him for fourteen years, and still his fear that he would do something in the natural, which was supposed to be of the Spirit, had kept him back from greater blessing and usefulness all this time.

A missionary of the very highest type, who was forced out of China by the war, told us that he knew two young men who had a call to the mission field, who were cultured, educated, and marvelously well qualified for the work, and yet they were held at home because they had not received the Holy Spirit. The Full Gospel organization to which they belonged would not send them out until they had received the Holy Spirit, with the Bible evidence of speaking with other tongues, and still it could not instruct them so that they could receive this gracious gift. What a tragedy! Since God commands all Christians to be filled with the Spirit (Acts 2:38; Eph. 5:18), it is unthinkable that His Word would not make the matter plain enough, so that a careful study of it would enable us to instruct the earnest seeker, so that he could at once receive the Holy Spirit, and thus obey the command.

Let us now go back for a little while and look more carefully at the scene described, where many were trying to help the one who was seeking the Holy Spirit. Let us remind ourselves again that the Holy Spirit is a person, and that He was sent as a gracious gift to God's people, not because they were worthy and deserved Him, but because they were hungry and needed Him. He is not given because we are holy, but He *was* given to help us to become mature, steady, fully developed Christians, which God wants us to be. Now for the man who said, "Hold on, brother." Is the Holy Spirit trying desperately to get away, so that the man must be told to hold on for dear life? Just what did the man really mean, who said, "Hold on"? Did either he or the seeker know what he was to do, which constituted "holding on"? The same question could be asked about the instructions to "Let go, brother." Should we give an instruction which we cannot explain clearly enough so that the man can obey it? Most certainly not. Take the instruction, "Now praise the Lord, brother, praise the Lord, He is coming in." Just what is the effect of this instruction, It is simply this: the seeker endeavors to do what he is told, so with vigor and enthusiasm he praises the Lord. Now he only thinks of praising the Lord in his own language, so when the Spirit is moving on his lips to put supernatural words there, he resists with all his might by going on to say his own words, but, by enough effort, he wins out, over-riding the Spirit's movings, and goes on speaking his natural language. How foolish; when we stop and carefully consider the situation. Both God and the man contending for possession of his lips to form the words which are to be spoken. Since God will not violate the principle of free moral agency (that is, force the man to act contrary to his own will), the man goes right on saying his own words, and God allows him to do so. Does not common intelligent tell us that the movements which the Spirit is causing on the man's lips and tongue are only suggestions to the man as to how God wants him to move his lips, to form the words which He wants him to speak? Then why not be obedient and move our lips as the Spirit leads, being willing to step out in faith, and let God have His way? Of course the sounds that will be made are only senseless noises to the natural man. He will not understand with his intelligence what he is saying. (Read I Cor. 14:14-15.) If he has to understand, there is no faith in that. Faith moves out on the suggestion of God with reckless abandon, leaving the results with Him. That is pleasing to God. It honors Him, and shows confidence in Him. So many have been afraid that they would grieve the Holy Spirit by making a mistake, and accidentally letting the flesh get in. Can we never come to a realization of the truth contained in I Sam. 16:7, "For the Lord seeth not as man seeth; for man looketh on the outward appearance, but the Lord looketh on the heart"? Is not it evident to every thinking person that our motive of heart is the thing God is interested in? It is sin, and only sin, on our part that grieves the Holy Spirit. It is impossible to grieve Him, as long as our motive is to glorify God, regardless of how many mistakes we make. Many children, in earnestly trying to help their parents, make mistakes which are costly, but no right thinking parent could punish the child, when it is evident that his motive was right.

Now look for a moment at the helper who says, "Now yield, brother, just yield." Here again, neither the instructor nor the instructed understands what is meant by yielding in most cases. The instructor, anxious to see the seeker receive the Holy Spirit, knows that he wants him to do something which will bring the desired result, but he doesn't know what that something is. What constitutes yielding can certainly be explained to the man, so that he will know exactly what to do, in order to co-operate with the Holy Spirit in what He is trying to accomplish. A little simple reasoning will make clear what yielding is, in the case where the Spirit is moving on the man's lips and tongue, until he finds it difficult to speak his own natural words. Yielding simply means that he is to stop all effort to speak his own words, refusing to utter a syllable which is the product of his own mind, but lift his voice, willing to make whatever sounds result from the movement of his lips and tongue which the Spirit is causing. Common sense will show us that this is yielding. Again we remind you that there is no scriptural warrant for telling people to lift up their hands and praise the Lord, in connection with receiving the Holy Spirit. This tradition, however, is so firmly rooted in the minds of most Full Gospel people that it is extremely difficult to get them to stop talking their natural language, when they feel the moving of the Spirit upon them. If, however, they will think the matter through, and bring their physical bodies, which are the temples of the Holy Spirit, into subjection by an act of the intelligence and the will, they will find that they can co-operate with the Spirit's movings and begin speaking a supernatural language as He is trying to get them to do.

Consider now the helper who questions; (when the seeker has come to the point of having stammering lips), "Now, brother, are you sure you have consecrated everything?" If it were not so tragic in the results, such a foolish question would be absolutely laughable, in a situation such as this. Let us remember that the Holy Spirit is a person and He either is in the believer, or He is not. The idea that He is just partly there, and partly not there, is entirely untrue and illogical. Now any supernatural manifestation of the Spirit, on the man, is positive proof of His presence. Stammering lips is just as much proof that the Holy Spirit is there in the man as a clear beautiful supernatural language. Both are the result of the Spirit's moving. Now since the Holy Spirit has come in, and is moving on the man in question, we have absolute proof that there is no spiritual lack which is hindering His coming. He has already come. The question is not, "Will the Holy Spirit come?" but the question is, "Will the man do his part in receiving what God has already given?" We have explained already what the man's part is in such a case. Simply to lift his voice and speak whatever sounds seem to want to come out, utterly disregarding what the sounds are. That is God's business. Let the seeker take care of his part and God will never fail to do His. If the man is willing to praise God with sounds which the Spirit causes his lips to form, he is acting faith, and God will honor it, and he soon will speak a clear language. An experience of the writer will illustrate this principle.

One day, while praying with a person in a large prayer tent at a camp meeting there came a lady who was unknown to us and stood watching. As soon as the person with whom we were praying began speaking in other tongues, moved by the Holy Spirit, the lady standing near, addressed us as follows, "I have been tarrying for the Holy Spirit for two years. I have shouted and praised God till I was hoarse many times, but as yet I have gotten nowhere, so far as receiving the Holy Spirit is concerned.

I am utterly discouraged and dejected, because of so many trials and failures. Do you think you could help me, sir?" I replied as follows, "Since you have shouted so loud and long try keeping still awhile. Kneel right down there by the bench, and don't, under any circumstances, say a word of English. Then when we lay hands on you, you are to RECEIVE the Holy Spirit as He moves upon you." She at once knelt down and we knelt down on the opposite side of the bench, facing her. We then laid our hands on her forearms, which were resting on the bench, and immediately the Spirit began to move upon her. Instead of beginning to speak a language at once, as I had expected, she began to speak one little single syllable word over and over again. She was so delighted that God had put one supernatural word on her lips that she did not stop to question what it was, or what it sounded like, but she just tossed it right back to heaven carrying her praise. With reckless abandon she looked up and shouted that one little word loudly and rapidly. As I knelt facing her, watching what was happening, God suddenly brought a vision before me, to my utter amazement. Right up out of the ground, beside the woman, there sprung a plant, like an enormous asparagus stalk. There were no leaves or limbs, but just a growing tip which shot up about one inch every time the woman said the one word that she was speaking. In wonder I watched this tip shooting up as it rapidly climbed toward the top of the big tent. Suddenly she spoke a second word, and instantly a limb shot out to one side. Then a third word brought another limb. And then just a free language began to flow like a river, with each word bringing a new limb on the tree. I could see nothing except the woman on her knees beside the most perfect, symmetrical, tree I have ever seen, and this heavenly stream of praise flowing out of her mouth in a supernatural language. When I recovered a little from my amazement, I said, "O, Lord, what can this mean?" And then God spoke to me. (I am very skeptical of these people who are always saying God told them this or that, and only a few times in my life can I say that God spoke to me, when it was as distinct and clear as a person speaking right beside you, but in this case I have no hesitation in saying that God spoke to me.) When He spoke He said, "Do you remember the story in the Bible of the hornets,

which I promised would drive out the Canaanites before the
children of Israel, after they entered into the promised land?"
(Read about them in Exodus 23:28-30; Deut. 7:20; Josh. 24:12.)
"Yes, Lord," I replied, "I remember about the hornets, but what
could those hornets possibly have to do with this woman and the
scene which is before me?" Again the Lord spoke and said,
"Just wait, and I will explain to you. I told the Israelites I would
not send the hornets and drive out their enemies all at once, lest
the land become desolate and the beasts of the field multiply
against them, but by little and little I would send the hornets
to clear out the enemies, and as they moved up by faith and
possessed the cleared land, I would send the hornets to drive
them back a little farther." I said at this point, "Lord, I am
beginning to get the light on this thing. I am beginning to see
what you are trying to teach me." Then He said, "I put one
supernatural word on this woman's lips and at once she possessed
it, and began to use it to express her praise and adoration. When
I saw that she would not stop to question, but joyfully use what
I gave her, I put another word on her lips, and when she did the
same with that one, I added another word." (During all this, the
woman was before me praising God in that wonderful new
language He had given her, and the vision remained unchanged.)
"Then when I saw she would joyfully use all I gave her, not
questioning in any way, I poured on this complete language
which flows with such beautiful freedom. The tree before you is
symbolical, in its complete symmetry and loveliness, of the perfection of the supernatural language I have given her." By this
time my wonder and delight knew no bounds and I sprang up
from my knees, praising God for what He had shown me. I am
sure that I got ahead of God that day, not waiting for a complete
understanding of the vision. However, during the next two years
I told many people about this experience and showed them that
if they would use what God gave them, even if they were only
stammering sounds, He would soon give them a complete language. As a result, many seekers received the Holy Spirit and
spoke with other tongues.

Two years later, sitting one day in my living room with my
Bible in my hand, I came to Isaiah 28 where we read in verses

11 and 12, "For with stammering lips and another tongue will he speak to this people. To whom He said, This is the rest wherewith ye may cause the weary to rest; and this is the refreshing: yet they would not hear." As I thought about it, I said to myself, "If this Scripture were written to fit most of the Full Gospel people's experience it would have to read, "This is the struggle wherewith ye may cause the weary to struggle'." But it did not say that, it said, "This is the rest wherewith ye may cause the weary to rest." I rose from my chair, laid my Bible down and started across the living room to where my wife was in the kitchen, to tell her about my thought on the subject. As I was about to the middle of the room, suddenly the vision appeared again, as I had seen it two years before. (Of course the woman was also part of the vision this time, and not there in the flesh as she had been before.) There was the wonderful tree, there was the woman on her knees in the shade of it, with the heavenly praises pouring out of her mouth, and her radiant face turned heavenward. It was all just as I had seen it two years before, and I should have recognized the woman instantly. Again God spoke to me. This time He said, "This is the rest wherewith ye may cause the weary to rest, and this is the refreshing," and then He added, "What could be a more beautiful picture of rest than this woman with radiant face, pouring out her praises to God, in a marvelous supernatural language under the shade of this beautiful tree?" Then it all disappeared, and I was standing speechless in the middle of the room. Words cannot describe how I felt. I cannot recount these incidents, even today after years have passed, without tears filling my eyes. Yes, this IS rest and the refreshing which we all so greatly need, and we need a fresh supply every day. Will we ever learn to relax and rest in the arms of the Lord, as a child, who has been hurt, relaxes and is comforted in the arms of its mother?

Now since the receiving of the Holy Spirit is entirely a matter of faith, what can we do that will help the one who has come to receive the Holy Spirit?

1. Help him see that God has already given the Spirit and that it is up to him to receive the GIFT now, and above every-

thing he is not to beg God to fill him with the Holy Spirit. All begging is in unbelief.

2. Lead him to see also that anyone who is saved is ready to receive the Holy Spirit. Someone might say here that Peter said in Acts 2:38-39, "Repent and be baptized everyone of you, in the name of Jesus Christ for the remission of sins, and ye shall receive the gift of the Holy Ghost." So how about being baptized first? We consent that this is the scriptural order, but we see that both the Apostle Paul and the people at the house of Cornelius, received the Holy Spirit before being baptized. We feel, however, that obedience in the matter of water baptism may cause faith to rise, especially if the candidate has seen that Scripture clearly. In fact he cannot receive the Holy Spirit before he is baptized, if he fully believes this order, and that he must comply with it. However, as soon as he is baptized, he can believe and receive the Holy Spirit.

3. Tell him that when hands are laid on him he is to receive the Holy Spirit. A little explanation is needed here. It is quite evident from the Scripture and from our experience that all do not have a ministry along this line, as God gives various ministries to his various servants. At Samaria (Acts 8:5-17) none received the Holy Spirit under Philip's ministry, but when Peter and John came down and laid hands on them they all received Him. Today some have this ministry and others do not, but we believe many more would have it if they asked God for it and believed. If you have no one at hand who has this ministry call in some one to help you who has. (Acts 10:5.)

4. Tell the candidate that he is to expect the Spirit to move on his vocal organs, and put supernatural words on his lips which he is to speak out in co-operation with the Spirit. Remember, the MAN speaks (lifts his voice) by an act of the will.

5. Tell him to throw away all fears, which he has gotten from foolish teachers, that he may get something false and spurious. Point out to him Luke 11:11-13, and help him to see that God promises he will not receive a substitute for the Holy Spirit, whom he has come to receive.

6. Tell the candidate to open his mouth wide and breathe in as deeply as possible, at the same time telling God in his heart,

"I am receiving the Spirit right now by faith." Absolutely insist that he shall not speak a single word of his natural language. Then, when you see the Spirit moving on his lips and tongue, after he has taken several deep breaths, tell him to just begin recklessly speaking whatever sounds seem easy to speak, utterly indifferent as to what they are. That is faith; as the person is lifting his voice and trusting God for the guidance. When he begins speaking tell him to go right on doing it, praising God with those supernatural words until a free clear language comes, and he has confidence and assurance that he has received the Holy Spirit. Some may say it is foolish to tell the candidate to open his mouth. If you feel this way, then read Psalms 119:131; 81:10. Also see Job 29:23 where there is a statement directly applying to the receiving of the Holy Spirit. (See chapter on "Instructions to Candidates" for more full discussion of this point.)

7. Don't have a crowd around, all giving instructions and getting him confused. If all present will either pray in the Spirit (*i.e.*, in other tongues, I Cor. 14:14-15), or pray quietly so as not to disturb the candidate they will greatly help him rise in faith. It is easy to see that when a dozen men are all praying aloud in their natural language, at once, the candidate hears a lot of things which he understands, and often it is not productive of unity. On the other hand, if the same twelve men are all praying aloud in other tongues, the praying is absolutely in unity, since One (the Holy Spirit) is guiding it, and it creates an atmosphere of faith in which it is easy for the candidate to rise in faith, and expect to do the same thing. The result is that almost always he will receive the Holy Spirit under these conditions. (Of course, if you want to stick to the old tradition, that it is spiritual lack which hinders the man, and God will fill him when He gets ready, none of these suggestions will help at all. Remember, however, that there is no Scriptural grounds for this deep rooted belief and tradition. It is entirely man-made and a dreadful hindrance to many earnest seekers.)

In recent years we have had hundreds receive the Holy Spirit when we gave them correct instructions, and fixed conditions around them which aided faith. We do not allow a lot of haphazard instructions, and so-called help, when we are in charge.

We tell people to either pray in the Spirit or keep still, and a great many have thanked us for this kind of help and instruction, which enabled them to joyfully enter into the blessed experience of being filled with the Holy Spirit.

We repeat again, in closing this chapter, the all-important instruction; that the candidate shall cast aside all thought of speaking his own natural words, which are the product of his own mind. Because of deep rooted tradition, we find that many will begin to talk in their natural language as soon as they feel the moving of the Spirit upon them, even after they have been shown that this is not the position of faith. If they do this we call everything to a halt, and tell them that they must stop even the whispering of their own words, if they are to speak with other tongues without a lot of struggling. A person can no more speak his natural language and also speak with other tongues at the same time, than he can speak two earthly languages at once. No one would be foolish enough to try to speak English and French at the same moment. He would put away all thought of speaking one when he began to speak the other. Why not use the same common sense in regard to speaking with other tongues?

Chapter XII

INSTRUCTION TO CANDIDATES FOR THE HOLY SPIRIT

The following is an address given before many hundreds of Christians, who have presented themselves as candidates to receive the Holy Spirit. Almost all of them have received Him when hands were laid on them, as they sat in their seats (Acts 2:2) and followed the instructions:

Now in talking to you good people about this matter of receiving the Holy Spirit, the first thing I would say is that I assume that you are all saved people, otherwise I would not expect you to be here. The Bible clearly states that the unsaved man cannot receive the Holy Spirit, so it would be useless for you to come to receive this precious gift of God, if you are not His children. Jesus said in John 14:16-17, "And I will pray the Father, and He shall give you another Comforter, that He may abide with you forever; even the Spirit of truth; whom the world cannot receive, because it seeth Him not, neither knoweth Him: but ye know Him; for He dwelleth with you, and shall be in you." Here is the clear statement of our Lord that the unsaved world cannot receive the Holy Spirit.

As children of God we must get certain teachings of the Word clearly in mind, if we are to reach out by faith and receive Him, whom the Father has sent to be our divine Comforter. The first principle that we must see is that the Holy Spirit is always spoken of as having been given as a free gift. In John 14:16 Jesus said, "And I will pray the Father, and He shall give you another Comforter." Again in Luke 11:13 we read where Jesus said, "If ye then, being evil, know how to give good gifts unto your children: how much more shall your heavenly Father give the Holy Spirit to them that ask Him?" Notice that these words concerning God giving the Holy Spirit, were spoken before Pentecost, but after that memorable day we do not find the Bible speaking about giving the Spirit to men. We have talked about God giving the

Spirit to men, or filling men with the Holy Spirit, but we are using incorrect terms. God GAVE the Holy Spirit on the Day of Pentecost, and from that day to this He has never given Him to a living soul. On the Day of Pentecost He was given to the whole church, for this dispensation, and now it is not a question of God's willingness to give the Spirit, but of the Christian's willingness to receive Him. After Pentecost we find the Word speaking about men receiving the Spirit, instead of God giving Him, but still it is always on the basis of GIFT. Peter said in Acts 2:38, "Repent, and be baptized every one of you in the name of Jesus Christ for the remission of sins, and ye shall receive the GIFT of the Holy Ghost." You see the word "receive" applies to the act of the one who gets something, and not to an act of the giver. In Acts 19:2 Paul said to those men at Ephesus, "Have ye received the Holy Ghost since ye believed?" He did not ask them if God had given them the Holy Ghost, for he knew that the Holy Spirit was given once for all.

Now gifts are received at once by faith, and are not worked for. If you work for something, or get good enough to merit it, then the thing becomes wages, or a reward for merit. No, my friends, everything we receive from God is on the basis of gift, and entirely by faith. In Gal. 3 we have several verses which make this very clear. Verse 2 says, "This only would I learn of you, Received ye the Spirit by the works of the law, or by the hearing of faith?" And, of course, the answer is, BY FAITH. Verse 5 says, "He therefore that ministereth to you the Spirit, and worketh miracles among you, doeth he it by the works of the law, or by the hearing of faith?" And again the answer is, BY FAITH. Then we have that wonderful statement in the 13th and 14th verses, "Christ hath redeemed us from the curse of the law, being made a curse for us: for it is written, Cursed is everyone that hangeth on a tree: That the blessing of Abraham might come on the Gentiles through Jesus Christ; that we might receive the promise of the Spirit through faith." Notice in each case it is by faith that we receive the Spirit. Let us return for a moment to verse 5, which we just quoted, and notice the word "ministereth". If your pastor stands up before you and preaches to you, he ministers the Word to you, or gives out the Word to you, and the same thought is here in this verse we are discussing. We have a demonstration of this in Acts 8:18 which reads, "And when Simon saw that through laying on of the Apostles' hands the Holy Ghost was given, he offered them money." We have heard the statement many times that no one can give the Holy Spirit to others, but here we have the clear statement that the Holy Spirit was given by the laying on of the Apostles' hands. And someone may say, "Yes, we admit that the apostles were able to minister the Holy Spirit to others, but who are you? You certainly are no apostle." To this we agree perfectly, but we would remind these people that the man who laid hands on the Apostle Paul, when he received the Holy Spirit, was an obscure disciple, named Ananias, who is mentioned only a few times in the Scripture. He was just a believer, such as you or I.

Since the Holy Spirit was given as a gift, therefore it cannot be true that we receive Him on the basis of our merit or our holiness. So often we have been led to believe that, as Christians, we must do this or that or the other thing, and get victory over certain evil habits, before we are good enough to receive the Holy Spirit. This is directly contrary to Scripture. To begin with, you have no righteousness of your own; you are no good, you never were any good, and you cannot hope to be any good, or have any righteousness other than the righteousness of Christ, which is by faith. You are no good, and I am just like you. The Apostle Paul said, "In me . . . dwelleth no good thing:" and I do not believe you are any greater than he. The sooner we realize this great truth, that we are hopelessly sinful, and no good, the sooner we will cast ourselves recklessly upon the Lord, and trust Him for the righteousness which is by faith. The moment that you receive Christ as your Saviour, you have credited to your account the perfect righteousness of Christ, and it is in His righteousness that you stand before God. All of your righteousnesses are as filthy rags, and it is only as we have the imputed righteousness of Christ that we have any standing with God whatsoever. There is no such thing as having a standing with God that is up today, and down tomorrow. You either stand complete in the righteousness of Christ, or else you have no standing at all, and are a lost sinner, clear on the outside. Christ took our sins that we might have His righteousness. Let us read Romans 4:5-8, and we will see that righteousness is by faith, "But to him that worketh not, but believeth on Him that justifieth the ungodly, his faith is counted for righteousness. Even as David also describeth the blessedness of the man, unto whom God imputeth righteousness without works, Saying, Blessed are they whose inquities are forgiven, and whose sins are covered. Blessed is the man to whom the Lord will not impute sin." In Romans 10:10 we read, "For with the heart man believeth unto righteousness; . . ." The Epistles abound with passages which show that the only righteousness which God recognizes is the righteousness of Christ, which is received by faith. Now since we see that we have a perfect standing with God, because of what Christ has done, let us not run away with the idea that we are perfect in our state of development. The building of Christian character is the process of a lifetime, and certainly there is much to be desired in the best of us. God did not give the Holy Spirit that we might receive Him because we had attained to a high degree of Christian character, but He gave Him that weak, faltering Christians might receive Him, and through His help, and guidance, and power, they might be shaped into the likeness of Christ. Remember this, whether it is the imputed righteousness of Christ that is credited to our account the moment we believe, or whether it is that righteousness which is built into us by the Holy Spirit day after day, in either case it is Christ's righteousness, and not yours or mine. I remind you again that you are no good, and that your only hope is in Him. If therefore God sees me clothed in the righteousness of Christ, His worthiness makes me worthy to receive anything that God has given to mankind.

So often we have heard this expression, "Oh, the Holy Spirit will never come into an unclean vessel." And with this statement we fully agree, but we would ask: what constitutes a clean, or an unclean vessel? A great many people have built up in their minds a set of standards, and if others do not measure up to those standards, then they say they are not clean. These people should remember the experience of Peter with the great sheet let down from Heaven in which were all those unclean beasts and creeping things. We will remember that God told Peter not to call anything unclean which He had cleansed. Any man that is saved, has been cleansed by the blood of Jesus, and is therefore ready in his present condition to receive the Holy Spirit. How illogical it is to admit that a man is saved, and then turn around and tell that man that he is not ready to receive the Holy Spirit. We all admit that if the man is saved, regardless of how weak and faltering a Christian he might be, he would go to be with the Lord if he should die. We admit that he is ready to stand uncondemned in the presence of God and all the holy angels, clothed in the righteousness of Christ, and surrounded by the beauties of Heaven. Now, how utterly illogical it is to tell that man that he is not ready to receive the Holy Spirit, which is only one of the means to the end that we have just described. How foolish it is to say that a man is ready for the end, which is Heaven, and tell him he is not ready for one of the means to that end, which is the receiving of the Holy Spirit here and now. All logic teaches us that the end is greater than any, or all of the means employed to attain the end.

Another thought which we wish to get into the minds of all is this, that we are here to receive a Person, and not just an experience. The receiving of the Holy Spirit is only learning the first simple lesson in co-operating with the moving of the Holy Spirit in our lives. The initial receiving is only important in this, that it constitutes the beginning of a fellowship with the Holy Spirit, which should be unbroken as long as God leaves us in this world. On the average we have made entirely too much of the initial experience, and entirely too little of the walk in the Spirit that should follow.

Let us notice that the only people who were taught to tarry for the Holy Spirit were those people (disciples) to whom Jesus gave this commission. They were told to tarry because the Spirit had not yet been given. Their waiting was not primarily a matter of getting ready to receive the Holy Spirit, but they were waiting for the coming of the Day of Pentecost, at which time the Holy Spirit was to be given in accordance with God's plan. Notice the Word does not say that the Holy Spirit came when they were fully ready, but it says, "When the Day of Pentecost was fully come, . . . they were all filled with the Holy Ghost," If it had been

God's plan to teach people to tarry for the Holy Spirit in this dispensation, which all Christians agree began at Pentecost, then we ask this most important question, why didn't Peter and Paul and the other early disciples teach people to tarry for the Holy Spirit? There is not the slightest record in the New Testament that anybody was ever taught to tarry for the Holy Spirit after the Day of Pentecost. How foolish it would be to say you are waiting and waiting for someone that is standing right beside you. The Holy Spirit is here and has been here ever since the Day of Pentecost; He is more anxious to possess you, and take up His residence in your body, than you are to have Him do so. No, my friends, to tell a man to tarry only suggests doubt. It suggests that the Holy Spirit is somewhere off in the distance, and I have to wait for Him. Let us realize that He is right here, and ready to be received the moment we will believe.

It is probable that some of you are saying to yourself, "Well, if spiritual lack is not the thing that is keeping me from receiving the Holy Spirit, then what is the hindering factor?" It certainly would not be surprising if you were thinking something like this, since we have been so often taught that God would give the Holy Spirit when we became good enough. I think, however, it will not be difficult to show you what has been hindering you from receiving the Holy Spirit, if you have been earnestly seeking, and have not yet received. I am sure you will admit that it is true that, if you have sought the Holy Spirit to any extent, you have felt His movings upon you, and since He is a Person, if you have felt His movings upon you, it is proof that He is there. Let us go back for a moment to Peter's statement in Acts 2:38, Ye shall RECEIVE the Gift of the Holy Ghost, and remember that that Word "receive" applies to an act on the part of the one who gets something. There are multitudes of people into whom the Holy Spirit has come, who have not yet performed their act of receiving Him. For instance, thousands of people have had stammering lips a great number of times before they ever came out clearly speaking with other tongues. The only reason they did not receive the Holy Spirit was because they did not understand exactly what He was trying to get them to do by His movings upon them; and that, good friends, is probably the reason why you have not received. You have not understood what the Spirit was trying to get you to do. One of the most hindering factors has been that we have been very careless in the terms, and expressions we have used concerning these things. We knew what we meant by the expressions we used, but very often those to whom we spoke did not. Another very misleading expression we use is this, we have said concerning the speaking with other tongues, which we all believe to be the initial evidence that we have received the Holy Spirit, that it is the Holy Spirit speaking through the man. For instance, if someone would stand up in a public meeting, and bring forth a message in tongues, and a stranger on the other side of the building looked inquiringly at the man next to him, this man quite possibly would say, "Now, brother, that is the Holy Spirit speaking through that man." Or very often it has been said to someone kneeling at the altar seeking the Holy Spirit, "Now, brother, just let the Holy Spirit speak through you." Expressions of this kind convey a mistaken idea to the listener. They convey the idea that, without any act of will on the part of the man, the Holy Spirit is just going to start speaking through his vocal organs. One pastor expressed it this way. He said that they were expecting that it would be just as if they swallowed a little radio, and then when the Holy Spirit got ready, He would turn it on and start it going. Now I have discovered in questioning many seekers for the Holy Spirit that most of them are looking for something about like what we have just described. They have been expecting the Holy Spirit to begin speaking through their vocal organs, without their having any part in it at all. This conception is entirely contrary to what the Bible teaches. Let us carefully read Acts 2:4 and see what it says. As we read I want you to notice that "THEY" is the subject of the sentence. It reads, "And they were all filled with the Holy Ghost, and began to speak with other tongues, as the Spirit gave them utterance." You see THEY is the implied subject in the second clause also; let's read it that way; And THEY began to speak with other tongues. It does not say the Holy Spirit began to speak; it says they began to speak as the Spirit gave *them* utterance: or as the Spirit gave them words to speak. If you will read almost any of the more modern translations of the New Testament, you will find that they make Acts 2:4 more clear than the authorized version. Weymouth's translation reads this way, "They were all filled with the Holy Spirit, and began to speak in other tongues according as the Spirit gave them words to utter." If I give you words to utter, I do not do the speaking. I simply tell you what to say, and you say it. The new Catholic translation, which is very excellent, reads this way, "And they were all filled with the Holy Spirit and began to speak in foreign tongues, even as the Holy Spirit prompted them to speak." If you were a child speaking a piece at a Christmas program, and you became frightened and got stuck, the teacher back behind the curtain, with the copy in her hand, would prompt you; but she certainly would not come out, and push you out of the way, and say the piece herself. No, she would tell you what to say, and you would say it, and get going again. These two translations, and many others, make clear what actually happens when the person speaks with other tongues. It is not the Holy Spirit doing the speaking, but it is the Holy Spirit supernaturally guiding the speaking. The man does the speaking by an act of the will just as truly as when he speaks his own natural language; the miracle is not in the fact that the man speaks: that is an act of the will; but the miracle lies in *what* the man speaks. What he speaks is entirely supernatural; he just speaks what the Spirit guides him to speak. Then you may say, "Well, if speaking with other tongues is simply Spirit-guided speaking, then how may I expect the Spirit to guide me?" That is a sensible question to have in your mind, and we should go carefully into this matter of the mode of guidance, so that you may recognize it when it comes.

A great many people have told me, after they did receive the Holy Spirit and spoke with other tongues, that the guidance for the speaking had been there for a long time, but, because of lack of understanding, or having mistaken ideas in their minds, they have not recognized it as such. One of the ways that the Spirit may guide you is this: somewhere down inside of you, I cannot tell you where, you will sense those strange words, and you will know exactly what they would sound like if they were spoken audibly. Many people have had this experience, but fear that they would do something in the flesh, as they have expressed it, has held them back from speaking these words, which the Holy

Spirit was prompting them to speak. There are two misunderstandings that have given Satan a powerful lever to stop people
from speaking with other tongues. They have believed first that
the Holy Spirit was going to do the speaking, which of course is
not true, and then they have been warned against the danger of
getting in the flesh. When the man begins to speak, Satan is right
there to shout in his ear, "Now stop, stop; you are getting in the
flesh. That is you doing that." So very often the man pulls himself to a stop, then Satan says to him, "See, see; I told you so. That
is you. That's not the Holy Spirit. You can stop whenever you
want to." A great many people have been stopped right at this
point, believing that these suggestions were from God, rather than
from the enemy of their souls. However, when the man understands that it is his part to do the speaking, and that the Spirit is
simply to furnish the guidance, he can go right on speaking without fear, realizing that this is only an attempt of Satan to stop him
from doing the thing that God wants him to do.

Another proof that it could not be true, that it is the Holy
Spirit who does the speaking, is that God has in His Word, in
I Cor. 14, distinct instructions as to when to speak with tongues
and when to keep silent. If the Holy Spirit did the speaking it
would be foolish of God to give the man instructions concerning
the control of speaking with tongues. The very fact that there are
definite instructions here concerning this thing, proves that it lies
within the man's power to obey them. We have had many people
begin to speak a clear, beautiful language immediately, as soon as
these points were made clear to them.

Another way that the Holy Spirit may prompt the man is by
supernaturally moving upon his lips and tongue to form words.
Let us examine, for a few moments, the different elements in
speech, and then we can see clearly what the Spirit is trying to
get us to do. All speech, whether natural or supernatural, has two
distinct elements to it; the forming of words with our lips and
tongue, and the producing of sound. You can form words with
your lips and tongue, and still not voice them. If you were sitting
in an audience and wanted to tell someone who was with you that
you were going home, you would not speak out and disturb others,
but you would look right at the person you wished to inform, and

form the words with your lips, and they could read your lips, and know what you said.

In natural speech the man's mind controls both of these factors. The mind causes his lips to move and form the words, and also causes the vocal chords to produce the sound to voice these words. But in supernatural speech this is not true. The man's mind controls only one of these factors. It is the man's part to furnish the voice and motive power to do the speaking, but it is the Spirit's part to furnish the guidance which directs the speaking. In other words, speaking with other tongues is an intelligent cooperation between the man and the Holy Spirit. If you will watch carefully what happens when the Spirit begins to move upon the person who is about to receive Him, as I have done in thousands of cases, you will see that the moving does not come in his throat. That is where sound comes from, and it is the man's part to lift his voice and produce it by an act of the will. You will see, however, that the Spirit will begin to move upon those parts of the vocal organs which form words. Very often the man will feel a tightening of those muscles in the axis of his jaws; those are the muscles that open the mouth, and the suggestion, or the prompting is—open your mouth. You can't talk with your mouth shut. And then you will notice that there is a supernatural quivering or fluttering on his lips, and if he opens his mouth you will see his tongue moving in strange ways. Now God doesn't do foolish things. These movings are for a purpose. They are simply promptings as to the way the Spirit wants the man to move his lips, to form the words which He wants him to speak. I think you can now see that if the man cooperates, he will move his lips and tongue to follow these promptings, and if he will lift his voice and begin to speak the words which result from these movements, he will be speaking in other tongues, as the Spirit gives utterance. We have laid hands upon hundreds of people, upon whom the Spirit was moving, telling them to recklessly lift their voices and speak whatever comes, trusting God for the guidance, and they have immediately burst forth speaking a supernatural language. Real faith always prepares the way, and gets things ready to receive that for which we have asked. You people before me are expecting to receive the Holy Spirit and speak with other tongues.

Therefore, faith dictates that you are to prepare to speak with other tongues as the Spirit moves upon you. Very often, however, the instructions and help that have been given to candidates have greatly hindered them from taking a position of faith and preparing to speak with other tongues.

Before I understood how mistaken I was, when someone would present himself as a candidate to receive the Holy Spirit I would say to him, "Now, brother, kneel down there. Lift up your hands and start praising the Lord." He only thinks of praising the Lord with his own natural language and so he starts off, all in good faith, praising God by saying glory and hallelujah, and other words of praise. Usually he has not been praising God long until he finds that it is difficult to say "glory". He does not realize it, but the Spirit is prompting him to move his lips contrary to the way his mind is moving them to form the word glory, and thus a conflict is set up. Here he is with his mind pushing in one direction and the Spirit urging in another. The result is that he begins to stammer and struggle harder than ever. His mind is all set on saying glory or other words of his own, and he does not realize that he is resisting the moving of the Spirit, who is trying to get him to speak supernatural words. And so the struggle goes on and on. But, I did not stop in my attempted help at this point. I could see that the Spirit was moving upon him, and I wanted to help him push over the hurdle, so quite probably I would shout, "Hold on, brother, hold on." One of my good assistants would say, "Now, just yield, brother, yield." While still another would insist, "Let go, brother, let go, let go." Then there was that one present who would tell him, "Let the Holy Ghost speak through you." And the poor candidate!! I have had dozens of them tell me that they became so confused by all of this shouting and contrary instructions, and so discouraged through trying time after time, and always having the same results, that they finally gave up altogether and quit seeking the Holy Spirit entirely. Almost all of these have joyfully received Him, when we have carefully explained to them what the Holy Spirit was trying to get them to do.

I have mentioned before the fact that real faith always prepares the way and gets ready to receive the thing for which we have asked. Let us pursue this thought a little farther. Let me give an illustration of what I mean by preparing the way. A man had a boy who was crippled, one leg being about four inches shorter than the other, so that the boy was forced to wear a shoe that was built up four inches. There was a meeting going on where they were praying for the sick, and the father took the boy to this meeting, that he might be healed, so that he would walk normally. Now what do you suppose the man did on the way to the meeting that constituted a step of faith, preparing the way to receive the healing? He stopped at a shoe store and bought a pair of normal shoes for the boy. Do you see what I am getting at? He got everything ready to receive the healing for which they were asking. The boy walked home healed, in the new shoes. I know a man who was prsent and saw this happen. Now you folks are here expecting to receive the Holy Spirit and speak with other tongues. Therefore, faith dictates that you get ready to speak with other tongues. Since you know that it is impossible to speak two languages at the same time, therefore, the only possible position of faith that you can take is this; I will not even whisper a word of my natural language. I am going to leave my lips free for the Holy Spirit to move upon, and when He does, then I am going to lift my voice and recklessly speak whatever words come, trusting God for the results. That is faith. Now, because of habit, you will probably find it difficult not to speak your natural language when you feel the moving of the Spirit, so you will have to discipline yourself to do the thing which constitutes a step of faith, and that is, refuse to speak your natural language or even whisper it.

One more thought I want you to get. It relates to the principle of inspiration. Many great men of faith have realized the principle that a person can quietly look up to God and breathe in divine healing by faith. The very word INSPIRATION means inbreathing, and the thought of breathing in the very breath of God appears a number of places in the Bible. Now I have discovered that the same principle that applies to divine healing, applies also to the receiving of the Holy Spirit. You can look up to God and open your mouth and breathe deeply, and by faith you can drink in the power of the Spirit. At first I told people to open their mouths slightly and just breathe in, worshipping the Lord as they did so, above all things refusing to beg God for the Holy

Spirit. He is here, ready to move in response to your step of faith. Recently I have discovered, through observation of a number of people, that those people who will open their mouths up wide will break forth speaking with tongues more clearly and easily than those who do not. Opening the mouth and breathing in constitutes a step of faith that God will honor. Shortly after I observed this truth, a sister pointed out to me what David says in Psa. 119:131, "I opened my mouth, and panted: for I longed for thy commandments." Here he really says: I opened my mouth, and panted after God. I have found that almost every one who has done this in our meetings, has received the Holy Spirit in a few minutes, and also has gotten a beautiful freedom to speak a clear supernatural language. Again, in Psalms 81:10 we have the instruction, "Open thy mouth wide, and I will fill it." But, some might say, these Scriptures do not state that they apply to this matter of receiving the Holy Spirit. Then let us look at one which surely does apply to this matter. Job 29:21-23 reads as follows, "Unto me men gave ear, and waited, and kept silence at my counsel. After my words they spake not again; and my speech dropped upon them. And they waited for me as for the rain; and they opened their mouth wide as for the latter rain." Here Job says they listened to me with their mouth wide open, just as people would do to receive the latter rain. Now it is agreed the world over, among full gospel people, that this great moving of the Spirit in these last days is the "latter rain" spoken of in James 5:7; Hos. 6:3; Zech. 10:1, etc. Hence we have a direct statement here as to how to receive the Spirit. Let us also consider the words of Jesus recorded in John 7:37-39, "In the last day, that great day of the feast, Jesus stood and cried, saying, If any man thirst, let him come unto me, and drink. He that believeth on me, as the scripture hath said, out of his belly shall flow rivers of living water. (But this spake he of the Spirit, which they that believe on him should receive: for the Holy Ghost was not yet given; because that Jesus was not yet glorified)." Here He literally says that we are to drink of the Spirit. Now, how does a person drink? First, he must open his mouth. Then he puts the cup to his lips, and draws in his breath. If Jesus did not expect us to receive the Spirit in this way, then why did He tell those who are thirsty for the

Spirit to come and drink? Too often we fail to take the Scripture in the simple way that it was intended to be taken. In I Cor. 12:13 we also get the idea of drinking of the Spirit. We have had a good number of people who have gone home after hearing these truths, and have returned to testify that they did as instructed, and received a glorious infilling of the Holy Spirit, speaking with other tongues as the Spirit gave them words to utter, while entirely alone with God.

If you will do this I can assure you that the Spirit will begin to move in a very short time. Then if you will begin to follow the promptings when they appear, opening and closing your mouth, and moving your lips as the Spirit guides you to do, you will find that the guidance will become more pronounced. Then if you will lift your voice, and begin to speak the words that are being formed on your lips by the guidance of the Holy Spirit, recklessly speaking whatever comes, giving no thought to the way it sounds, you will receive a lovely clear language. When you once start to speak, do it recklessly, hilariously, trusting God to do His part. That is faith, and that pleases God. Determine that when you once start you will not let anything stop you from going ahead with the speaking until you get a clear, free language. Remember, Satan will fight you. He will try to make you believe that you are making up the words yourself, or that you are imitating someone else. He will say, "Now, you are getting in the flesh and that is dangerous." Pay no attention to any of these suggestions of the devil, knowing that God looks on the heart, and if your motive of heart is to please God, then you can go determinedly forward to complete victory. I see no reason why we should spend more time discussing this matter. Let us now look up in faith and worship God, drinking in as the Bible suggests, and ye shall receive the gift of the Holy Ghost.

Chapter XIII

QUESTIONS AND ANSWERS

In the following chapter we purpose to state a number of questions which are often asked concerning the receiving of the Holy Spirit, and our relations to Him, and then answer them as the Word of God teaches. It is probable that in answering these questions we will repeat, in part at least, statements made in other parts of the book, but we feel that this will not be amiss, as many of these points should be repeated for emphasis.

1. Can a person, who has received the Holy Spirit, speak with tongues at any time he wills to do so?

Answer: Yes, if he clearly understands what the Word teaches. It is made very clear in I Cor. 14 that the man controls the speaking with tongues by an act of the will. However, if the man does not understand his part in this matter, he will not be able to speak with tongues, as fear that he will do something which he ought not to do, will hold him back from exercising this lovely gift. We have a great many who have received the Spirit, but had no freedom to speak with tongues in their private life. When shown what the Word teaches on this subject, almost all of them began to speak with tongues and rejoice in the blessings which followed. (See chapter on "Why Speak With Tongues?")

2. If the Spirit-filled person can speak with tongues at will, then where does the supernatural element come in?

Answer: The miracle is not in the *fact* that the person speaks with tongues; that is an act of the will, but *what* the person speaks is the part which is miraculous. He can go on speaking with tongues as long as he wishes, but he has absolutely no control as to what the words are, which he speaks. This is where the miracle comes in. Speaking with tongues is not the Holy Spirit speaking, as so many have believed, but it is the person speaking as the Spirit miraculously guides him, giving him the words to say. Notice how Acts 2:4 is worded in Weymouth's translation, "They were all filled with the Holy Spirit, and began to speak in other tongues, according as the Spirit gave them words to utter." Most all of the modern translations of Acts 2:4 make it clear that the man speaks as the Spirit prompts him or gives him words to speak.

3. Is not speaking with tongues, and manifesting other gifts of the Spirit, a proof that the person is living a life of holiness and consecration to God?

Answer: Most certainly not. Many have stumbled over this point, and often they have backslidden completely when they have seen people talk with tongues and still not live right. There are a number of cases recorded in the Bible where people, who were not living as they should, manifested genuine gifts of the Spirit. (See Num. 23:1-12; I Sam. 19:20-24; I Kings 13:11-32; John 11:49-52.) Paul makes this point clear in I Cor. 13. He does not once suggest that the gifts mentioned there were not genuine, but certainly does point out that the people manifesting them may not have love in their hearts. Gifts can never be a proof of holy living, as the person is always a free moral agent, and has to make his choices in line with or against God's will, after he receives gifts of the Spirit, just as he does before he receives them. However, let us not forget one thing: Gifts of the Spirit lay upon the possessor an added responsibility to live a holy life, but, sad to say, he does not always live up to his responsibility.

4. Is it ever proper for the leader of a meeting to stop people from speaking with tongues in the meeting?

Answer: Yes. There are many conditions under which the leader is not only justified in stopping people from speaking with tongues, but it is his responsibility to do so. There are plain instructions in the Word concerning these things and we should go by the Word. "Let all things be done unto edifying." (I Cor. 14:26.) "Let all things be done decently and in order." (verse 40.) "But if there be no interpreter, let him keep silence in the church; and let him speak to himself, and to God." (verse 28.)

Let those in authority remember that these things can be done in a gentle loving way, which will not embarrass the one who is being instructed. If possible it is best to deal with, and instruct these people privately, as timid people are often so

crushed by any public rebuke that they are put in a state of
bondage which is most difficult to overcome. We do not want
to stop them from manifesting spiritual gifts, but rather encourage
them along this line as the Bible does. However, we do want these
manifestations to be brought forth in line with the Bible instructions.

The following experience of the writer will illustrate this
point. Soon after organizing the church, which we pastored for
seventeen years, a young lady began coming to our services, who
had a most beautiful gift of tongues and interpretations of tongues,
but she had no instruction as to when or where to manifest her
gifts. The result was that very often, in a Sunday morning service,
she would burst forth with a message in tongues, and then give a
lovely and entirely Scriptural interpretation of the message. It
was beautiful and would have been most uplifting if it had been
rightly timed, but usually it was right in the midst of the prayer
which the pastor, or someone else was leading. We believed in
praying for definite things, and expecting definite answers, so we
often had a number of requests, which we were unitedly bringing before the Lord. Our minds would be concentrated upon the
things for which we were praying, when suddenly the bomb
shell would burst, and everybody's attention would be diverted
from the petitions we were lifting up to God, and we would
begin listening to the lovely message in tongues, and the equally
lovely interpretation of it. When this was finished the poor person,
who had been leading the prayer, would do his best to gather up
the scattered threads and bring the minds of the people back to
the petitions. You see, all was confusion because things were not
correctly co-ordinated, as God's Word directs. We prayed about
this matter much, feeling that something must be done, but we
realized that the young lady was a timid soul, who could be easily
hurt by any public rebuke.

We, therefore, went to her home and addressed her something
like this: "Now Sister, you have a lovely gift from the Lord, and
we want to encourage you in the use of it. We feel that we can
help you to make it more glorifying to God by giving a few
instructions as to when and where to manifest it." At this point
she burst into tears, and sobbed out that she was glad we had

come to instruct her. She said she had never had any teaching along this line, and that she was afraid she would be quenching the Spirit if she did not give forth the message as soon as she felt His moving within her. We explained that if she would just hold back until a suitable time came in the service, then the people's minds would not be drawn away from the prayer, and also they would be in better condition to receive the benefit of her message. In addition, we pointed out to her the fact that the Holy Spirit would not be grieved or quenched by her waiting for the proper time to give her message, but that He would be pleased, and the message would gain in spiritual power and blessing.

For a period of many years following this instruction, this sister often gave beautiful and uplifting messages, which were a real source of inspiration and help to all who heard, and never once did she give one at an inopportune time. If we had given this sister a public rebuke her gift probably would never have been manifested again, and the assembly would have suffered a great loss.

5. What is the fire spoken of by John the Baptist in connection with the coming of the Holy Spirit? (Matt. 3:11-12; Luke 3:16-17.)

Answer: Our answer to this question may not be very popular with those who have interpreted the fire to be that unction, enthusiasm, and zeal which often accompanies the receiving of the Holy Spirit. To some, sad to say, the fire is loud shouting, loud praying, fast talking and being very demonstrative whether there is any real blessing of God or not. We often hear people say something like this: "I want to see those who receive the Holy Spirit really the get the fire too." These people mean the enthusiasm and activity just spoken of. Now we believe that any sincere person, who will carefully read the passages given, will see that the fire mentioned is something entirely different. We are not depreciating the unction and divine enthusiasm which Spirit-filled people have, as that is most valuable, when it is truly of God, but this is not the fire John speaks of in connection with receiving the Holy Spirit. It seems to us that both Matthew and Luke explain the fire in the verse following the statement that believers shall be baptized with the Holy Ghost and fire. (Matt. 3:11-12; Luke 3:16-17)

Here they compare the work of the Spirit to the threshing and separating of the grain from the chaff; the grain being put in the barn, and the chaff burned with unquenchable fire. Now if we are to be our best for God the chaff must be burned out of our lives, to leave the grain clean and pure for His use. It is not the easy things in life which purify, but it is the trials, hardships, sorrows, reproaches, sicknesses and disappointments which God uses to shape us into His image. The fire spoken of here is the fire which consumes and purifies. It is not comfortable to the natural man to submit to this fire, for it means death to self and self interests, and the flesh rebels against this process. No one ever goes far in becoming like Christ without submitting to these things which, like fire, consume the chaff and leave the grain for the Master's use. Yes, "Ye shall be baptized with the Holy Ghost and fire."

6. Must not the person be fully yielded to the Spirit after receiving Him, if his experience is to be deep and abiding?

Answer: Yes, indeed. It is after we have received the Holy Spirit that the real test of obedience and consecration comes. Sad to say, many receive the Spirit, and then push Him off into some obscure corner of their spiritual house, reserving most of it for their own pleasure and purposes. The beautiful fruit of the Spirit can never develop normally in the life of the person who is not fully yielded to Him. We cannot, by our efforts, make ourselves a bit more holy, or good, or Christlike, but we can yield ourselves fully to the indwelling Spirit, and He will mould us and shape us into the likeness of Christ. Nothing but full and complete yieldedness to the Holy Spirit will ever bring about the beautiful Christlike character which God wants to see in us.

7. Do people receive as deep and lasting an experience when they receive the Holy Spirit at once by the laying on of hands, as they do when they tarry and wait a long time for Him?

Answer: Yes, indeed. The fact is, we feel that they are in a much better position to go forward in faith than those who beg and tarry a long time. Receiving at once by faith is far more glorifying to Christ than working and struggling to receive the Spirit, which magnifies the man and his works, and depreciates the grace of God. The same principle is involved, which is brought out in Eph. 2:8-9, "For by grace are ye saved through faith; and that not of yourselves: it is the gift of God: not of works, lest any man should boast."

The experience of a man of our acquaintance will illustrate. This man was saved about thirty years ago, and during the first twenty years of this period he would seek the Holy Spirit earnestly for some time. Then in discouragement he would get cold and careless and lose interest in church. He also would get back to chewing snuff again. Then after a year or two of this he would be aroused by some evangelist and go through a season of desperate seeking for the Holy Spirit. Again in disappointment and discouragement he would sink back into his old life of indifference. At the end of more than twenty years of going around this cycle, he came back from another state to visit in his old home community, where I was pastor of the church. At this time he was in the bottom of a spiritual depression, and bound by the snuff chewing habit. On Saturday he brought his week's supply of snuff and put it under the floor mat of his car, as he was ashamed for any one to see it. The next morning he came to church with his wife, who was a very steady Christian, and also came back in the evening. Before entering the service in the evening, he threw away a large chew of snuff just as he entered the building. After the meeting, when almost all were gone, and his wife had gone out to the car, he stayed behind to bid me good bye, as they were leaving the next day, to go back to their home in another state. Calling him by name, I said, "C---------, you have gone too long already without receiving the Holy Spirit. Now is the time to take a step of faith. Kneel down right now, and as we lay hands on you, the Holy Spirit will move upon you, and when He does you co-operate by giving Him your voice." He did as instructed and in only a few minute's time he was freely speaking with other tongues. I told them good bye and they drove away to go back to their distant home.

Ten years later we saw them again. I went to hold meetings in a city a few miles from where he lived and felt led to look him up. I found he was manager of a large seed cleaning plant, so I went there to find him. I entered the plant and saw him standing with his back to me. Soon he turned and saw me and his first words were these, "Brother, my heart has never lost the glow"; and although he was covered with the dust from the seed cleaning machines, still that heavenly peace on his face shone through it all. In these ten years he had never wavered. The old snuff was thrown out and never came back. He is getting old now but his advanced age is beautified by the loveliness of Jesus. A few weeks after our meeting in the mill, he came on a Sunday morning to our revival meeting, and gave a testimony that thrilled the hearts of the audience and glorified Jesus, pointing out that it was His grace, and not our goodness, which makes it possible for us to receive the Holy Spirit.

Yes, dear reader, receiving the Holy Spirit simply by faith glorifies Jesus far more than all your laboring and begging and struggling could ever do.

8. Is it not possible for a Christian to receive false tongues or a false spirit when seeking to receive the Holy Spirit?

Answer: When people ask that question we know that they have somewhere come in contact with one of these "faith blasters" who go about making statements which have no foundation in Scripture. When we suggest to earnest Christians that they may get something false, when seeking more of the fulness of God, we sinfully dishonor God and His Holy Spirit. Where, we ask, is there the slightest suggestion in the Bible that the Christian, whose heart longs for more of God, may get false tongues or a false spirit? If such a thing could happen, it would have to be true that, either God was too careless and indifferent about the welfare of His children, or else He was too weak to protect them from the power of the enemy. To suggest either one of these things is horrible, as it makes God out to be either a puny weakling, or a careless monster.

If we will take the Scriture as our guide, we will see that it flatly contradicts such a wicked thought. Luke 11:11-13 points out most emphatically that God will not give His children a worthless or harmful substitute when they come to receive the Holy Spirit. The very essence of the character of God is love.

Can any sane person conceive of a loving Father, who is all wise and all powerful, giving His hungering child a false and harmful substitute? There are hundreds of Scriptures which point out that God seeks only the welfare and blessing of His children.

Cast away forever the repulsive idea that God would allow His child to receive something false and harmful when seeking to be obedient in this matter of receiving His Holy Spirit with the supernatural signs accompanying. Pay no attention to anyone who goes about suggesting such unscriptural things which only promote doubts and fears.

9. Are all the things which people do, when moved upon by the Spirit, to be classified as true manifestations of the Spirit?

Answer: No, indeed! Most of the things which people do, when moved on by the Spirit, must be classified as human reactions to the moving of the Spirit. Only the nine GIFTS of the Spirit listed in I Cor. 12:7-10 can correctly be classified as manifestations of the Spirit. Very often violent demonstrations and loud screaming, result from the moving of the Spirit, because the person either deliberately resists, or does not know how to yield to His moving. Usually it is that the person does not know how to yield, so that there may be a true manifestation of the Spirit, rather than a deliberate resistance. Teaching from the Word will help people to yield to the Spirit more fully.

10. Is it not true that Jesus will fill the seeker with the Holy Spirit when He gets ready, and sees that the seeker is prepared to receive Him?

Answer: This is about as far from the truth as it can be. To begin with, God GAVE the Holy Spirit at Pentecost, and from that day to this He has been here. God has never given the Holy Spirit to anyone since that day. His part in this matter was finished at that time. The Holy Spirit was given that all SAVED people down through the ages might receive Him, if they would reach out in faith. Let us remember that faith comes from teaching from the Word, and during most of the ages since Pentecost there has been little, or no, teaching on the subject until recent years. It is as foolish to tell a man that God will fill him with the Spirit when He gets ready, as it is to tell someone that God will save him when He gets ready to do so. Today it is not a question of God's willingness to save any man, or fill any Christian with the Holy Spirit. Those questions were answered at Calvary and Pentecost. It is now a question of the man's willingness to receive the salvation which was provided by Christ's sacrifice, or to receive the Holy Spirit, who was given at Pentecost. It is up to the man to receive God's gifts by faith, which were given at Calvary and Pentecost.

11. Is not God demanding the impossible, when He commands all Christians to receive the Holy Spirit? We have seen many earnest believers tarry for years and finally give up in despair. Can you explain this?

Answer: Surely the experience of many people would make it appear that God is demanding the impossible, but if He really did so, He would be a cruel despot, instead of the loving Father that He is. Now the reason that these people seek for the Holy Spirit, and do not receive Him, is because they have never clearly understood what the Bible teaches on the subject. It can be easily proved, from many different angles, that spiritual lack is not the hindering factor. This point has been covered in other parts of this book. The trouble with these people is their failure to yield their bodies to the Spirit, and not the Spirit's failure to move on them. Practically all of them will testify that the Spirit moves on them when they wait on Him. Their failure to yield consists in their persistence in speaking their own natural language when the Spirit is trying to put supernatural words on their lips. There is not the slightest scriptural grounds for telling people to lift up their hands and praise the Lord in connection with receiving the Holly Spirit, and still dozens have told us that they have been urged, and almost forced by earnest helpers to hold up their hands until their arms were so tired that they could think of little else but their aching muscles. Have we come to the place of doing penance in order to receive the gift which has already been given?

12. Why do you teach people that they need not "tarry" for the Holy Spirit when Jesus taught His disciples to do so?

Answer: Jesus taught His disciples to "tarry" because the Spirit was not yet given. (John 7:37-39.) After the dispensation of the Holy Spirit was ushered in by His coming, on the Day of Pentecost, there is not the slightest evidence in the New Testament that anyone was ever taught to "tarry" for the Spirit. If it were God's plan for us to be taught to tarry for the Holy Spirit in this dispensation, then why, we ask, did not Peter and Paul and the other apostles teach their converts to tarry? Instead, they laid hands on them and they received the Spirit at once. (See Acts 8:17; 9:17; 19:6.) We find that when converts are dealt with scripturally almost all will receive the Spirit as they did in the early church.

13. Cannot we see Pentecost repeated if we get sufficiently in earnest?

Answer: Definitely NO. Pentecost was the day when the Holy Spirit was sent into the world, in fulfillment of Jesus' promise to pray the Father to give another Comforter. The church was born on that day, and the dispensation of the Holy Spirit was ushered in. The Holy Spirit will not be sent again. He is here and has been since that memorable Day of Pentecost, and He will remain here until His mission, preparing a bride for Christ, is finished. We may, however, look for, and expect, all the power and blessing of the early Church to be repeated in the closing days of this church age. In fact, we would be failing God if we were not earnestly praying to this end. We believe that all the supernatural powers manifested in the beginning will again be seen in the church in the last days of this age.

14. Did not the disciples have to be in harmony (one accord) before the Spirit came on the Day of Pentecost? (Acts 2:1.)

Answer: We have often heard sermons where the preacher drew heavily on his imagination concerning the perfect unity which had come among the waiting disciples before the Holy Spirit could come upon them. According to most of the modern translations of Acts 2:1 there is no mention of their being in perfect harmony. The "one accord" mentioned in the Authorized Version simply means that they were all in the same place at the same time. We quote from Weymouth and also from the revised Catholic version 1941 Ed. "Now, in the course of the Day of Pentecost, they had all met in one place" (Weymouth); "And when the Days of Pentecost were drawing to a close, they were all together in one place" (Revised Challoner-Rheims version).

The coming of the Spirit on the Day of Pentecost was entirely dispensational in character. The Bible does not say that the Spirit came when the disciples were ready, but it says that He came when the Day of Pentecost was fully come.

15. We have often heard that Christians cannot be instructed so that they can receive the Holy Spirit at once. Is this true?

Answer: Most emphatically NO. The Holy Spirit WAS GIVEN at Pentecost, given in all His fullness, and He has never been given to a single soul from that day to this. God's part in giving the Spirit to the church was finished on that day. From that time to this, it has not been a question of God's willingness to give the Spirit to any Christian. It has been a question of man's willingness to receive the Holy Spirit. We do not read about God giving the Spirit after Pentecost, but we find the apostles enquiring of people whether they had RECEIVED the Spirit or not, (Acts 19:6) and instructing them to *receive* the Spirit. If God commands us to receive the Holy Spirit, and He does, (Eph. 5:18; Acts 2:38-39; Gal. 3:2, 5, 13-14) then when we understand what the Bible teaches we can receive Him at once. We can instruct people how to receive the Holy Spirit just as successfully as we can instruct them how to be saved. (See chapter on "Dealing With the Candidate For the Holy Spirit.")

16. Is there always an act of the will on the part of the man when a person speaks with other tongues supernaturally?

Answer: Yes. If the Spirit spoke through the person without his will or consent, then God would be violating the principle of the free moral agency of man. Unfortunately, in the Full Gospel movement, we have been careless in the terms and expressions we have used, and it has caused much damage. We have constantly used the expression, "The Holy Spirit speaks through the man," which is misleading. The actual fact is that the man speaks as the Spirit supernaturally guides him. If we will read Acts 2:4 carefully, we will see that it teaches that the Spirit gives the words but the man utters them, thus the Spirit guides the speaking. Now, if the man would not lift his voice and speak by an act of will, then there would be no speaking done.

The fact that there are instructions in I Cor. 14 as to when not to speak with tongues and when to do so, is ample proof that the man controls the speaking by an act of will. If we read Acts 2:4 in the more modern translations, we will see that many of them make it more clear than the Authorized Version that the man speaks as the Spirit guides him. In the lifting of the voice the man takes an active step of faith, and the Spirit honors it by putting the supernatural words on the lips of the speaker. If anyone who speaks with tongues will carefully analyze his experience he will see this truth.

Now we grant that many have been so taken up with joy of being filled with the Sprit, that they did not stop to consider what really happened when they spoke with tongues. On careful examination they will find that their experience lines up with the Word, and that they control the speaking by an act of the will. If the man can *will* not to speak with tongues, and carry out that purpose, then if he does speak with tongues, it is because he does not will not to do so, and therefore wills to do so.

17. Is it necessarily true that those who have gifts of the Spirit also have much of the fruit of the Spirit?

Answer: NO. The fruit and gifts of the Spirit do not necessarily go together. In I Cor. 13:1-2 the Apostle Paul points out that people may have gifts and not have love, which is the very essence of the fruit of the Spirit. Christian character is the result of the development of the fruit of the Spirit in our lives. Now the maturing of fruit is a slow process which is going on constantly in our lives, faster or more slowly according to the measure of our yieldedness to the Holy Spirit. It is the fruit of the *Spirit* in which we are interested: not the fruit of our labors. Only the Spirit can cause Christ to be formed in us, and that is what God is looking for.

Now gifts, on the other hand, come to the possessor in a moment of time. They are given that we might be established. (Rom. 1:11.) They are a means to an end and that end is that we might be like Jesus. However regrettable it may be, it is true that many people receive the Holy Spirit, and gifts of the Spirit, and still do not continue to yield themselves to Him, so that He may have freedom to work in their lives, and cause Christ to be formed in them, and surely it is He alone who can make us like Jesus. We must remember that people are free moral agents after they receive the Holy Spirit just as much as they were before, and it is after we have received Him that the real test of yieldedness comes.

If we will think of this life of ours as a spiritual house, made up of many rooms, we may be able to get the correct picture of the situation. We may give the Spirit complete freedom to control and order what goes on in every room, or we may push Him off into some small closet or attic, and keep the other rooms for our own selfish purposes. Now some would say, "Oh! the Holy Spirit never would remain under those conditions. He would leave at once, if treated that way." No, my friend, you are mistaken. That is just the time of all times that He would stay, realizing our great need of His guidance and love. If He left there would be nothing to draw us back to a place of willingness to give up our selfish ways, which only lead to a barren, fruitless life. Surely He is grieved, by our unwillingness, but He will never leave as long as He sees that there is a chance to bring us back to the place of surrender and blessing. God loves us with an everlasting love, and will do everything in His power to make our lives fruitful and happy.

18. Will people have as great temptation after receiving the Holy Spirit as they did before?

Answer: Yes. In fact they will probably have greater trials and tests of faith, but, thank God, they will have the precious Holy Spirit to help them over the difficult path. It is in the meeting of hard trials, and overcoming them, that we grow spiritually. A life of ease and freedom from tests of faith never makes sturdy soldiers of the cross.

Too often people have been led to believe, by the testimony of others, that life will be a bed of roses after they receive the Holy Spirit. Some have seemed to think they were boarding a spiritual roller coaster which would roll steadily on without difficulty, until it carried them triumphantly through the pearly gates. We should never lose sight of the fact that Jesus was led by the Spirit into the wilderness, to be tempted of the devil, immediately after the Holy Spirit came upon Him when He was baptized by John in the Jordan River. Let us remember that the servant is not greater than his Lord. It has been proved to us, by asking for a show of hands in many audiences, that a large part of people have greater tests of faith after receiving the Holy Spirit than they ever had before. Many of them had a great spiritual battle immediately after receiving the Spirit. If Satan can defeat us at once, after we receive the Holy Spirit, he has gone a long way toward our permanent defeat.

We feel that Christians should be warned that probably they will be attacked by Satan right after receiving the Spirit. If this is done, they will be prepared for the attack and ready to meet it with the Word and the Spirit which is in them. Many have come to us telling us how they suffered great defeat soon after receiving the Spirit, because they had not been given Scriptural instruction as to how to meet the enemy of their souls. For this reason we are very insistent that all who receive the Holy Spirit shall not stop until they get real freedom in speaking with other tongues. If people have this complete liberty in speaking with tongues day by day, it will be a divine source of power with which to meet the enemy, who will do all he can to rob them of their new source of power and blessing.

19. Has not the Holy Spirit come upon many people who have never spoken with other tongues?

Answer: Yes. It is undoubtedly true that this is the case. In fact it is always true that the Spirit comes upon the person before he speaks with tongues, and in many cases it has been years after the Spirit came upon the man, that he first spoke with other tongues. Acts 19:6 will throw light on this question. "And when Paul had laid his hands upon them, the Holy Spirit came on them; and they spake with tongues, and prophesied."

Now the unction, or anointing, to speak with tongues is there as soon as the Spirit comes upon the man, but very often the man does not understand what the Spirit is trying to get him to do. Therefore he may go on seeking for years, not knowing that the power to speak with tongues is there, if he would only take a step of faith and do it. We have great numbers of people who say, after receiving the Spirit, and speaking with tongues for the first time, "Why I realize that I could have done that long ago if I had only known what the Spirit was trying to get me to do."

You see, the lifting of the voice and speaking, as the Spirit gives the words, constitutes a step of faith which can be taken as soon as the Christian sees clearly what the Bible teaches on the subject. The person who has never spoken with tongues, and thus has failed to do his part in receiving the gift which has already been given, will not have the benefit from the Spirit's presence that he would receive if he provided, by faith, a channel through which the Spirit can manifest Himself.

Let it be noted here that we have not said that the man has RECEIVED the Holy Spirit before speaking with other tongues, as his act of faith, in speaking with other tongues, is the act which indicates that he receives the gift. After Pentecost we do not find them talking about God giving the Holy Spirit to people, but we find them talking about men RECEIVING the Spirit whom God has given. There is an act of receiving on the part of the man, and the act is his speaking with other tongues. (See also the chapter on "Reasons For Speaking With Other Tongues.")

20. Is it true that the Holy Spirit can be imparted to Christians by faith, by the laying on of hands?

Answer: YES. Acts 8:1-19 makes this very clear, but it would suggest that not all have this ministry. Here we have the story of Philip going to Samaria and having a great revival which moved the whole city. There were all kinds of wonderful miracles of healing and deliverance from demon power, and yet, not one received the Holy Spirit under Philip's ministry.

Let us look at verses 14 to 19 which read as follows, "Now when the apostles which were at Jerusalem heard that Samaria had received the word of God, they sent unto them Peter and John: who, when they were come down, prayed for them, that they might receive the Holy Ghost: (For as yet He was fallen upon none of them: only they were baptized in the name of the Lord Jesus.) Then laid they their hands on them, and they received the Holy Ghost. And when Simon saw that through laying on of the apostles' hands the Holy Ghost was given, he offered them money, saying, Give me also this power, that on whomsoever I lay hands, he may receive the Holy Ghost." A great number had been saved, as it tells us they were baptized in water, and we know that Philip would not baptize the Ethiopian eunuch until he declared his faith in Jesus as Savior (verses 37-38). Acts 9:10-17 will help us. It reads as follows: "And there was a certain disciple at Damascus, named Ananias; and to him said the Lord in a vision, Ananias. And he said, Behold, I am here, Lord. And the Lord said unto him, Arise, and go into the street which is called Straight, and enquire in the house of Judas for one called Saul, of Tarsus: for, behold, he prayeth. And hath seen in a vision a man named Ananias coming in, and putting his hands on him, that he might receive his sight. Then Ananias answered, Lord, I have heard by many of this man, how much evil he hath done to thy saints at Jerusalem: and here he hath authority from the chief priests to bind all that call on thy name. But the Lord said unto him, Go thy way: for he is a chosen vessel unto me, to bear my name before the Gentiles, and kings, and the children of Israel: for I will show him how great things he must suffer for my name's sake. And Ananias went his way, and entered into the house; and putting his hands on him said, Brother Saul, the Lord, even Jesus, that appeared unto thee in the way as thou camest, hath sent me, that thou mightest receive thy sight, and be filled with the Holy Ghost." Here we have an obscure Christian disciple, named Ananias, such as you or I, going to Saul of Tarsus and laying hands on him that he might receive the Holy Ghost. He was not an apostle, and is only mentioned a very few times in the New Testament, and still God used him to lay hands on the great Apostle Paul.

We have had many hundreds in our meetings who have been brought to a place of faith, by teaching from the Word, so that, when we laid hands on them they received the Holy Spirit, and began to speak with tongues, as the Spirit gave them utterance, ("Gave them words to utter." Weymouth). Many will begin to speak with tongues instantly when hands are laid on them.

We realize that many have taken the position that no one can impart the Holy Spirit to others, but the Bible makes it clear that this is not correct. Galatians 3:5 would also indicate that the Spirit is ministered (imparted) to others by faith. We would do well to take God's Word on this subject, rather than believing the traditions of men.

21. Is it true that the man must always make the first move when co-operating with God, to bring about a miracle?

Answer: Yes. If we go through the miracles of the Bible we will find that the man always did something which constituted a step of faith. For example: (Ex. 14: 16-21) Moses stretched out his rod over the Red Sea and then the water was divided; (II Kings 2:14) Elisha struck the water of Jordan with Elijah's mantle, and then it separated; (II Kings 2:20-21) he threw salt into the bad water of Jericho and it was made good; (II Kings 4: 40-41) he put meal into the pot of poisoned pottage and then it was good to eat. Now there was nothing supernatural about Moses stretching out his rod or Elisha striking the water with the mantle, or any of the other of these acts which man performed. Each was an act of the will which constituted a step of faith, and that is what God will honor.

Now in this matter of speaking with other tongues there surely is a miracle, and the miracle is brought about by a step of faith. It is the Spirit-filled man's part to lift his voice by an act of will, trusting the Spirit to give the words, and He never fails to do so.

22. If we do not receive the Holy Spirit because of our righteous character, then why does the Bible say that God will give the Holy Spirit to those who obey Him?

Answer: The obedience here spoken of cannot be other than the obedience of faith, for we know that no one, from the time of the children of Israel in the wilderness up to the present, has perfectly kept God's laws (except Jesus). If it were on the basis of obedience, it would have to be absolutely perfect obedience, since God demands perfect holiness. No one has this except in Christ, being clothed in His perfect righteousness, which is by faith and faith alone. It is on the basis of His righteousness obtained by faith, that we are worthy to receive the Holy Spirit or any other gift from God. Romans 10:10 says, "For with the heart man BELIEVETH unto RIGHTEOUSNESS." (See also Rom. 3:21-22; 10:3-4; Gal. 3:2.)

23. If all Christians should speak with tongues, as you teach,

then why the question in I Cor. 12:30, "Do all speak with tongues?" because the answer is evidently "No."

Answer: We agree perfectly that the answer to this question is NO, but we believe a careful consideration of the context will explain the apparent contradiction. In the first part of the chapter, verses 8 to 10, we have a list of gifts of the Spirit to individuals in the church, and "divers kinds of tongues" is one of the gifts listed. In the last part of the chapter (verses 28-30) a list of men is given, who minister under the power of the Spirit, and who are equipped with the gifts of the Spirit. The questions in verses 29-30 show this clearly, although the last part of verse 28 looks to the casual observer, like a list of gifts. The Apostle Paul is not illogical enough to mix men and gifts in the same list, especially when writing under the anointing of the Spirit. Here he is talking about ministering the gift of tongues, *i.e.*, bringing forth a message in tongues in the public assembly, which is to be interpreted. (See I Cor. 14:5, 13, 27.)

Many people who speak with tongues in their prayer life, never give a message in tongues in a public meeting, to be interpreted. In this sense all do not speak with tongues. If the reader of the Scripture does not see this distinction he finds that the Word contradicts itself. Paul says in I Cor. 14:5, "I would that ye all spake with tongues." Both Weymouth and the new Catholic version say, "I should like you all to speak with tongues." Jesus said, "These signs shall follow them that believe . . . they shall speak with new tongues." (Mark 16:17.)

In every record in the book of Acts, where it tells of people receiving the Holy Spirit, and anything is said about the supernatural evidence accompanying their receiving of the Spirit, it always says they spoke with tongues.

Now if this question, "Do all speak with tongues" is talking about the speaking with tongues as an evidence of receiving the Holy Spirit or in private worship, then there is a hopeless conflict in the Scripture. To the spiritually minded man who thinks clearly, it seems to us that he cannot fail to see that this question refers to the ministry of tongues in the public assembly.

Chapter XIV

SOME LETTERS RECEIVED BY THE WRITER

We print the following letters in part, or in their entirety, to show the tragic effects of some mistaken ideas and teachings upon the lives of those who have been misled by them, and the happy results of getting these same people to clearly understand what the Bible teaches concerning these things. Our only object in printing them is to help others who have had similar experiences, believing that a great number will get encouragement from them to reach out by faith and receive the blessed Holy Spirit.

The first letter we print describes so perfectly the experiences of many others that we feel it is well worth reading. Of course the details are different in every case, but the general principles are the same. We have inserted our comments between the paragraphs as we wish to call particular attention to certain points as the letter is being read.

Vancouver, B.C.
Sept. 1, 1948.

Dear Brother Stiles,

Just how much your ministry has meant to me is difficult to express. After nearly twenty years of struggling and seeking for the baptism of the Holy Spirit, God knew my need and sent you to me.

My parents came into the Full Gospel in the early years, and were instrumental in commencing the Pentecostal Church in ------------, Alberta, nearly thirty years ago. So I was brought up in it, and have always attended church whether I cared to or not.

My folks believed in bringing their children to Sunday school and also to church.

At the age of seven I spent practically the whole winter in bed with one ailment after another, which included pneumonia and weeks of fever. Mother was afraid my time was short, so would read Bible Stories and tell me about salvation and Heaven every evening. The year before she had suffered with severe gall stone attacks, and during one of these had begged me, along with my younger brother of three, to pray for her. I refused, saying, "How do I know that there is a God?" for my childish mind could not conceive how a being could exist without having some beginning. So one night as Mother talked with me I looked up with simple childlike faith and gave my heart to Him. Immediately, before my startled gaze, I saw the Lord before me. He stood with arms outstretched toward me and one foot extended as though stepping down to where I lay. The beauty of His raiment fairly dazzled my eyes, and I was struck with the singular loveliness of His countenance. The expression was so tender, so loving, and so kind. It took place in an instant of time. Being so young I knew nothing of visions, but, as I began to tell Mother of what had just taken place, she realized what had happened. Through the years that have followed never once have I doubted the existence of God or His supernatural power and manifestations. Even when the heavens have seemed as brass the memory of this would flash into my mind.

The following summer I was baptized in water and soon after began to seek for the infilling of the Holy Spirit, but at an early age, barely into my teens, began to become discouraged. About that time God seemed to especially visit our Assembly, and quite a number were receiving the experience. Finally I gave up, and the Pastor stopped me one evening and asked why I wasn't up seeking with the rest. Out of hurt pride I flippantly remarked that I'd be up there with the rest if I wanted it. He gave me a good admonition right there on the seriousness of the statement just made. A fear gripped me that I had committed the unpardonable sin, and it tortured me for years whenever I went up to seek. How I rued those words, for the desire for all God had to give me never left me.

Then in my last years of high school and the years that fol-lowed I lost out with God. A love for the world crept in. Suffice it to say that I marvel at the love of God and His patient dealing and striving with erring ones.

This young lady told us that she can now see very clearly that her backsliding was caused directly by the discouragement resulting from struggling to receive the Holy Spirit and failing to do so. We constantly meet people who tell us that they had a like experience.

During this time the principal of one of our prominent Canadian Bible Colleges came to town and I was interested. I wanted a change and felt it would mean a new start. Dad was particularly anxious for me to go and sacrificed to send me. I began to seek the Lord again and asked forgiveness for the years of backsliding, naturally expecting a joy and assurance similar to the night I was saved. But it did not happen, and finally I had to take my stand on the Word, and say, "Lord, I believe your prom-ise—if we confess our sins He is faithful and just to forgive us our sins, and to cleanse us from all unrighteousness." That brought the assurance, and during the three years at college I conscien-tiously studied and sought God, for I realized that He had a defi-nite plan for my life, and it could never be fulfilled until I had received what He had in store for me.

So often people have been led to believe that they must have certain feelings in order to be sure they are saved. This is a great mistake. Salvation is by faith, and joyful feelings are the result of faith; *i.e.*, simply believing what God's Word says. When we believe the Word then assurance and joy will follow.

Leaving college I entered gospel work with my room mate who had received the Holy Spirit. We filled in at several small churches, the last of which was my home Assembly. The people were simply marvelous to us and we appreciated the way they stood behind us. It meant everything to me to be in the Lord's work, and yet I never forgot my lack and the feeling of inade-quacy. Hours of prayer always preceded my speaking as I realized I needed twice as much help as one who had received the Holy Spirit. Also I had discovered what it was like to speak with no liberty, and wanted to feel the presence of the Holy Spirit brood-

ing over the service. The Lord was very gracious to us and would take all fear and nervousness away the minute I got up to speak, for I had to rest in Him. Then in our after meetings I had to seek the Holy Spirit and thus was unable to help anyone else. You can imagine what it was like.

Only those who have experienced it can know the awful inferiority complex and depression which results from preaching the Full Gospel message and struggling at the same time to receive that, about which they are preaching. We have no record of such a thing in the Bible, and it is a shame that we should not be able to help any earnest Christian to receive the Holy Spirit at once. We have proved in hundreds of cases that practically all Christians who present themselves as candidates, will receive the Holy Spirit the first time they come, if they are correctly instructed from the Word.

When we left . . . (my home town) I resolved never to speak again until I had received the Holy Spirit, which perhaps was a mistake, but I had come to the place where I felt I could not go on. How could I lead anyone into a place of confidence and trust in God, when I could not touch Him for my own need?

All through the years my father spared no time or expense in helping us to attend camp meetings and conferences. I knew it hurt him when I didn't go to the prayer room, and although I loved listening to the Word being unfolded, a dread of the after meetings began to grip me. Many times I have stumbled down the saw dust aisles of tents and camp auditoriums with eyes filled with tears, and sobs scarcely controllable, crying out to God to reveal the hindrance.

One night in particular I left the tabernacle on the camp grounds at Sylvan Lake, my arms numb from being extended. Whenever I put them down for a rest, someone would whisper in my ears that God wanted men to pray with holy hands lifted up toward Him; also it would bring the blessing more quickly. A well meaning sister had put her hand on my head and shook me till I could take no more: nearly knocked me over and I would not fall under the power unless God put me there. That happened once when I was a very young girl, and the shock of acting a lie never left me. Standing out under the trees, with the stars twink-

*ling down in the darkness, and the shouts of prayer and praise
coming from the tabernacle, I looked toward Heaven, and extend-
ing my hands, I cried to God from a heart of chaos, defeated,
discouraged and bewildered, asking Him to reveal in some way
the hindrance in my life.*

Could any thinking person doubt the sincerity of this young
woman in her crying to God to show her what was hindering
her receiving the Holy Spirit? This kind of a situation represents
God as being meaner than the man who would whip his child
unmercifully, and then refuse to tell him why he was punishing
him. God has commanded us to receive the Holy Spirit, and
here this young lady, along with thousands of others, is in an
agony of soul because she does not know what is hindering her
from receiving Him for whom her heart earnestly longs. These
people have been led to believe, by our general teaching that
spiritual lack is what is hindering them from receiving the Spirit
and still you can never find one earnest seeker who knows what
is hindering him. Can any sane man believe a loving God would
treat His children so? Now God does not treat His children so,
but unscriptural teaching has gotten people in this awful condition. All of such people will joyfully receive the Holy Spirit
when taught according to the Word, and dealt with according to
biblical practice.

In a recent tour of eight months in Canada, over one thousand
received the Holy Spirit, many of whom had tarried for years
and years. This young lady was among them.

*A very close friend of mine one day told me that several of
them had been talking about me in their cabin and could not
imagine what was holding me back. "There must be something in
your life, Esther. Perhaps it's your private prayer and devotional
time. You may not be spending as much time as you should."
Things in my life that I had long ago confessed began to trouble
me and I never went to pray but what I cried for forgiveness and
tried to straighten out my life.*

What a tragedy that seeking to find out the hindrance to receiving the Spirit, had driven her to keep bringing up the old
sins which had been honestly confessed. The teaching that the
Holy Spirit will be given when we are spiritually prepared drives

people to this very thing, and thus they dishonor God by failing to believe that the sins they have confessed are really forgiven.

Another friend, a gospel worker, told my Mother that she believed I would never receive until I said yes to a call as a missionary to India, which she knew I had. She also said the same to me. When Mother spoke to me about this, I answered, "Mother, do you think God would reveal to her what He had ordained for my life, and not say a word about it to me?" However, I began to wonder if it was lack of consecration which was the hindering factor. Personally India would have been a hard pill to take. So then I had to come to the place where I would say yes to even that. Had I received then, it would naturally have meant to me that God wished me to go to India.

How many people's lives have been blighted by others claiming to have revelations from God as to His plan for their lives. God can speak to you if He wants you to do certain things.

Someone else told me to get my mind off tongues. "What are you seeking, tongues or the Baptizer?" Another brother told me that as he was praying the Spirit would lift whenever he thought about tongues. So whenever I felt a prompting of the Spirit, and words would become hard to form, my mind naturally thought of tongues, and I would stop.

How utterly illogical is the reasoning of the person who will say that speaking with other tongues is the initial evidence that a person has received the Holy Spirit, and then tell the seeker that he is not seeking tongues, but he is seeking the Holy Spirit. This at once suggests that the Christian may receive tongues without receiving the Holy Spirit. This same person who made such statements to the seeker would shout and praise God the moment the seeker began to speak with other tongues. We want to repeat the statement made elsewhere in this book that it is a libel upon the character of God to suggest that He would allow His child to receive something false and spurious when earnestly seeking more of God. Read Luke 11:11-13. The actual fact is that the Bible encourages us to seek to speak with tongues, as this is the only one of the nine gifts of the Spirit mentioned as being edifying to the one who exercises the gift. (See I Cor. 12:31; 14:2, 4, 5, 14, 15, 17, 18 & 39.) Every Spirit-filled person should speak with tongues every day of his life. This young lady, along with many others, was held back from receiving the Holy Spirit for years by the fear of over emphasizing tongues. If there were a danger here God would have warned us of it. All that such suggestions accomplish is to fill the mind of the seeker with doubts and fears.

Finally I stopped seeking, for the only time I could pray and feel spiritually refreshed, was when I prayed for other things and forgot about receiving the Holy Spirit. When my pastor stopped me one Sunday night with the words, "You are a candidate, Esther, aren't you?" I replied, caught off guard, "Well, yes, I guess I am." "Why aren't you in the prayer room?" So I told him I had no hope or faith that I could ever receive. I had gone so often I could go no more. He spoke to me for awhile showing me that I was on dangerous ground, and begged me to reconsider and go right into the prayer room, where my friends would all rally round and help me. I walked out, bitter and shaken, for I realized I was on dangerous ground.

This has been the experience of thousands. We find it everywhere we go. These people had faith for a little while when they first sought the Holy Spirit, but they soon passed over the crest and started down hill. From that point on every time of tarrying, and failing to receive, brought them to a new low level of faith. Finally they stop seeking altogether, as they have no hope of receiving. Then, to top it all, they are accused by others of being indifferent, or of harboring secret sin in their lives. Any logical thinker can see the ruin and devastation which this situation brings in the lives of many earnest hungry seekers.

I had filled my time with activity. My room mate and I spent hardly an evening at home, and when we did we had friends in. But when her hours at work were changed, and I would come home alone to the apartment a restlessness would seize me, and a longing for God, and fear of what was happening to me. I was out of the work, no hope of being used of God, no spiritual growth, but rather spiritual stagnation setting in, for that naturally follows when we are not advancing in this Christian walk. I had given up my Sunday School class of girls as my pupils were receiving and I felt unqualified to continue. In fact I refused to take part in any, form of religious service. As I thought of these things, I would fall on my knees and sob out to God to undertake for me, and in some way to satisfy the hunger of my soul.

One Sunday afternoon I slept too long, so dashed around the corner to a little Full Gospel Tabernacle where a former Bible College teacher of mine was pastoring. After the service I made myself known, and he told me of an evangelist named Mr. Stiles who spoke and dealt on the baptism of the Holy Spirit. He expected him to come, and told me to contact any candidates that I could and bring them along. I just couldn't tell him I was one myself, but resolved that if this man could help me I would seize the opportunity.

In the meantime I went on my holidays, and, on the Saturday evening after my return, went out to the park for a bit of relaxation with a friend of mine. She asked me if I ever intended going back into gospel work again, to which I replied that it depended on whether or not I received the Holy Spirit. But I did not believe I ever would. Walking home that night, thinking about these things, I wondered if the evangelist had come yet, and resolved to find out. After the church service next day, friends drove us home and remarked that Brother Stiles was speaking that afternoon. I was there, but didn't know what to think. As he laid hands on the candidates he told them not to say one word in English, but to open their mouths and begin to speak in tongues which was an act of faith. It horrified me, as I had always thought God would suddenly switch the languages with no help from me whatever. I went again that night and saw a friend of mine receive. The following Tuesday night a Christian Missionary Alliance man received, and I knew it was real.

During that week I scarcely slept at night due to the mental struggle I was going through. "It's now or never," I told my room mate. "If I don't receive now I'm through with Pentecost. It will have to be a church where it is not preached, as this thing cannot haunt me any longer." Thursday night as I went up for prayer my heart beat in expectancy and yet fear struggled with hope. I had been disappointed so often: was there even a spark of faith left to reach out and take the gift? I left that night with no assurance; true I had spoken words that were not English but the *struggle in my soul was too great. I walked around town until I was sure no one I knew would be on the bus, and while walking decided I would speak in tongues, so opened my mouth and began to speak a few words over and over.*

Here she had come to a place where she could not continue in a church which taught the receiving of the Holy Spirit, and have the fact haunting her continually that she had not received the Holy Spirit. There are thousands who have left this blessed Full Gospel movement for this very reason. Sad to say, a large part of our Full Gospel people just assume that these people are compromisers, and not willing to pay the price of going on with the group which is looked down upon by some.

The next night I came back and as the evangelist talked to me after the service, faith began to rise and on Saturday night as a portion of scripture was read (Gal. 3:1-5) and I listened to messages in prophecy, tongues and interpretation, assurance began to flood into my soul.

When I awoke Sunday morning and lay in bed praying in tongues, the presence of the Lord became so real and near, that I felt that if I reached out my hand I would feel His garment. Things seemed so different, the burden that oppressed me was gone, no condemnation, no doubt, no fear, discouragement and defeat were gone. I felt washed and clean and absolutely free. Peace and quietness, where there had been turmoil, reigned. Surely the Lord had been good to me. Nothing in me has merited any of His favor, but I am so grateful that He continued to deal with me.

Looking back over these years of my youth which have been largely wasted due to lack of proper teaching as to the receiving of the Holy Spirit, my prayer is that I might be used to help someone else who is stumbling over the same things that I stumbled over. Also may my testimony help altar workers in their dealings with seekers.

Brother Stiles, may God abundantly bless you and your precious wife.   *Your sister in Christ,*

(signed) Esther Sorensen

If the reader of this sad story which, thank God, finally ended in blessed victory, will carefully analyze the whole thing, he will see that it was all brought about by a very few fundamental errors. The teaching that,

1. We must tarry for the Holy Spirit in this dispensation.
2. The Holy Spirit will be given when the candidate is properly prepared.
3. The Holy Spirit will DO the speaking in other tongues.
4. There is a danger of getting in the flesh.

Again we remind you that the only righteousness which any of us can have, is the righteousness of Christ which is by faith, and if we are saved, regardless of how faltering Christians we may be, we stand complete before God, clothed in Christ's perfect righteousness. This, and this alone, makes us worthy to receive what God has for His children. May we ever honor God by trusting Him for righteousness, for Christ is our righteousness; praise His wonderful name.

Davidson - Hay Hospital
Port Angeles, Washington
May 20, 1948

Dear Brother and Sister Stiles:
Praise God from whom all blessings flow!
The Lord surely has been good to me all these ten years since I have had salvation, but He seems sweeter and nearer since I received that wonderful gift—the baptism of the Holy Spirit— about a month ago. He whom the Lord sets free is free indeed, and bless God, I do feel free, the first time in my life.

I have wanted the baptism for so long, have prayed earnestly, went to meetings everywhere I could, tarried some, although my work as a registered nurse kept me from tarrying all night, as I was told to do. I finally came to the conclusion that I wasn't saved at all, or I would have gotten the baptism, so when you people came to Sequim, I decided I'd have a real confessional, see what was the matter with me, and have you give me some advice and help, but bless the Lord, you told me instead, that regardless of how much I tried to be good, or how much good works I did, I was no good anyway, only in Jesus, because "He paid it all."

I began to see myself as I really am, realized I must depend wholly upon Him for everything, and after throwing myself entirely upon Him, the sweetest peace came over me, and I began speaking in other tongues.

Wish I could tell you more about that peace and love that came into my heart and is still there, thank the Lord. Naturally, I am quite shy of people, and would have to know folks a long time before I could love them, but now everyone looks good to me, even unsaved people. I feel so sorry for them, and keep thinking how Jesus died for them, too. I have a real burden of prayer for the unsaved, and I'm going to keep praying for them until Jesus comes.

Christian love to you and Sister Stiles. I hope you will be this way soon again.

Sincerely,

(signed) Mrs. Edna Broughton, R.N.

This letter was printed to show that Satan, who is the accuser of the brethren, will use the fact that people have failed to receive the Holy Spirit as a means to make them believe that they are not saved. Very often this is the final blow which throws the person into complete confusion and discouragement. We have asked in a number of audiences: How many here have either backslidden completely or been brought to the verge of backsliding by the discouragement resulting from seeking the Holy Spirit and failing to receive Him? In every case where this question has been asked, a considerable number of hands have been raised indicating that this had been the person's experience. In one Bible School almost half of the students testified that at some point in their seeking, they had come to this sad state of discouragement. Now these, with whom we have come in contact, are those that weathered the storm, and finally got back on their feet spiritually, but what about the great number that have gone down under the impact of this thing, and have failed to ever get straightened out? We have had people tell us of friends and acquaintances who are not serving God today because of this very thing.

Portland, Oregon,
June 26, 1946.

I thank God that you came my way and taught me that I had to use my vocal organs to do the speaking, as the Holy Spirit prompted me instead of the Holy Ghost doing it all, and speaking through me. (signed) *Mrs. Marie Stout.*

Portland, Oregon,
June 20, 1947.

I have thanked God many times that He ever gave me the privilege of hearing you minister. For six years I had wandered around in doubt and unbelief concerning the Holy Ghost, and at times the devil told me I wasn't even saved. I was looking at myself and seeing all my mistakes, and going by feelings instead of faith in Jesus. I was trying ever so hard to live a perfect life and it seemed like I was going down hill in spite of all I did.

I was never satisfied with the baptism of the Holy Ghost because I was very ignorant of what the scriptures have to say concerning Him. I never spoke in a clear tongue until you, Brother Stiles, laid hands on me: then I immediately spoke in a clear tongue and have done so ever since, and it is now easier for me to pray in tongues than in English: and this past year has just been wonderful for me. I can truly say I have enjoyed my Christian life this past year, as I never did before. It has certainly been joy and peace for me, for I never realized a person could enjoy themselves so much in this life.

When I began speaking other tongues after you laid your hands on me I wondered if this would truly last, but I can truly say it does last. I have been satisfied, and not one time have I ever been discouraged in my Christian experience this past year, since I know my position is in Christ and not my own personal holiness. Grace, such marvelous grace; I did not know God loved me so. I I could write on and on of the wonderful things the Holy Ghost has revealed to me during this year. Only eternity can reveal what the truth has done for me.

May God continue to bless you, Brother and Sister Stiles.

A sister in Christ,
(signed) *Marie Stout.*

We print the short testimony of Mrs. Marie Stout, and the letter she wrote to us a year later to show the effect of teaching people that all Spirit-filled persons should speak with tongues every day in their private prayer life, and also to show the result of the person getting a clear vision of their standing in Christ. A short time ago (April, 1949) we ministered in the church where Mrs. Stout and her husband are members, and she is today a happy victorious Christian.

Bethel Church, Fifteenth & G Sts.,
Modesto, California,
June 19, 1948.

John E. Stiles,
Oakdale, California.
Dear Reverend Stiles:

I want to write you this letter in appreciation of your wonderful ministry this last week in Bethel Church, Modesto.

Inasmuch as we have been busy night and day, I not have the chance to tell you personally at the time just how much your words of faith meant to me as an individual, and to the church as a whole.

A sweeping revival in the deeper things of God has broken out in the church as the result of your three Bible studies on the gift of the Holy Spirit. Tweny-nine (29) of our very best folk wonderfully received the mighty infilling of the Holy Spirit in those few short days . . . and best of all, it has revolutionized their lives. They are reading the Bible, testifying, and in turn are creating a hunger in other lives with whom they come in contact.

After hearing your three messages I want to say "They were solid Bible Gospel" Keep up the good work. Your constant elevation of Christ and the Bible . . . faith and grace is a thrill!

I trust that many doors will open to you in your ministry of encouraging folk in the deeper walk! We at Bethel will always treasure your time with us.

Sincerely yours in Christ,
(signed) Donald G. Weston
Minister of Bethel Church, Modesto, since 1934.

Excerpts from

SASKATCHEWAN DISTRICT NEWS

Pentecostal Assemblies of Canada

SASKATOON—It has been our privilege to have Brother and Sister J. E. Stiles of Oakdale, California, with us for three days. Bro. Stiles was worked almost to exhaustion, as in the Bible school and at Elim he ministered for more than eleven hours a day. Blessing followed a scripturally sound teaching. Unfolding of the Word that brought faith and understanding to the listeners which resulted in about twenty-five receiving the Holy Ghost. His presentation of the bestowal and operation of the gifts of the Spirit was definitely sound, and we know will profit all that heard. Brother and Sister Stiles left Friday for Winnipeg, where they are holding meetings in Calvary Temple.

Sunday morning at Elim—Evangelist gone, but the revival continues. While the service was in progress, there was a prayer meeting going on in a Sunday School room, where eleven boys and girls received the Holy Spirit. Sunday night in the prayer room, three young women received the Holy Spirit as they knelt in prayer. Two of the latter number are school teachers attending Normal. Hallelujah and praise the Lord!

C. H. Stiller, District Superintendent.
January 20, 1949.

The letters from pastors and the excerpts from the Saskatchewan District News, printed herein, are inserted to show the effect on churches and workers when they get clear, simple and scriptural teaching along the lines indicated.

In our recent trip to Canada, where we went to stay two months, and stayed eight months instead, we conducted campaigns in twelve churches from Vancouver, B.C., to Winnipeg, Manitoba. In these eight months more than one thousand people received the Holy Spirit with the Bible evidence of speaking with other tongues. Surely all the praise is due to our glorious Lord, for we are nothing without Him. We have nothing good inherent in ourselves to commend us to God. Along with the Apostle Paul we must say, "In me (that is, in my flesh) dwelleth no good thing." Romans 7:18. Surely God's plan for us leaves us no place for boasting, for everything we receive from Him is just another proof of His matchless grace toward sinful men.

As we bring out the second edition of our book we feel that it would be well to tell a little about the effect the reading of the first edition has produced in the lives of the readers. We are getting a constant stream of letters telling how people, who have tarried and struggled for years to receive the Holy Spirit, have joyfully received Him when they read this book and came into a clear understanding of the part the Spirit expected them to play. Many who have received the Spirit in years gone by, did not have freedom to speak with tongues in their private life, and as they read this book, they got light and understanding which made it possible for them to reach out in faith and take that freedom for which their hearts have longed. Others have had questions concerning these things which have troubled them for years, and they write in to say that this book has cleared away all their difficulties.

We are also finding that many people entirely outside the ranks of the Full Gospel movement are getting light from a new angle, and as a result, they joyfully receive the Holy Spirit and speak with other tongues as He gives them guidance.

We could fill a book the size of this one with testimonies of the light and liberty and blessings that have come as a result of getting the truths contained in it. The following letter will give a good idea of the kind of letters which we receive:

January 1st, 1951.

"Dear Brother Stiles:

I have one of your books on the Gift of the Holy Spirit, which I ordered from Shreveport, La. I think it is the most wonderful book that I've ever read; it is the answer to all my problems. I have been seeking the Holy Spirit for three years, and was just ready to give up when I saw this book listed in the "Voice of Healing" magazine. Now I find, after reading your book, that I have been speaking with tongues all the time but just did not believe. I feel that a great burden has been lifted off of me. I cannot find words to tell you what this book has meant to me. I think it is the most helpful book ever written.

Please send me two more books, which I will give to friends of mine, who, like myself, have been seeking for a long time and have become discouraged.

May God bless you for your good work in helping poor souls find their way to the Lord. Please pray for me.

Your sister in Christ

(Signed) Julia Smith,
1025 Hendrie St., Detroit, Michigan."

In one large city a young lady school teacher was in our meeting for one week. She then left to take a teaching position in a school in a distant state. When she arrived the pastor of the church where she decided to attend, asked her to take charge of the mid-week meetings while he was gone on a three weeks' vacation. At first she declined, and then she thought of our book which she had brought with her from home. With the desire to try out the principles it taught she re-considered and said she would conduct the meetings.

At the first meeting she told the people about the meetings she had attended, and then read to them excerpts from the book. She then asked those to come forward who wished to receive the Holy Spirit. Five responded and received a wonderful infilling that night. We later heard that everyone in the church had received the Spirit before the pastor returned from his vacation.

We received a letter from an army officer who was so moved by the effect of this book that he ordered twenty more books to distribute; and later sent another large order.

We print this letter to show the results of teaching the principles which are taught in this book.

"Dear Brother Stiles:

We thank God that He permitted you and Mrs. Stiles to come to the .... Gospel Tabernacle. With your kindly and careful instructions my wife and I received the baptism of the Holy Ghost the first time we heard you, over a month ago. We had been seeking this experience for many, many years. Such a blessing would in itself have been cause for rejoicing, but you and Mrs. Stiles have so carefully and painstakingly taught us a new way of living, which brings such great comfort, that we are living more victorious lives.

When I was teaching in college I very seriously assumed the responsibility of making the difficult portions as simple as possible. You and Mrs. Stiles have succeeded in simplifying some of the great fundamentals of our Christian faith. Both of you have inspired us by your daily lives.

We also wish to praise God and to thank you and Mrs. Stiles for helping us appreciate the great blessings we have through our Pentecostal faith, namely, salvation for our souls, healing for our bodies and the baptism of the Holy Ghost for victorious living. Your emphasis on the importance of receiving the Holy Ghost and the necessity of Him dwelling in our bodies has helped our thinking very much.

For many years my wife and I sought the baptism of the Holy Ghost. Both of us were hindered and discouraged by what appeared to be emotional displays that did not seem orderly and inspired. We felt that speaking in tongues was an indication of spiritual growth, but usual methods of tarrying lacked the reverence and orderliness that seems to be true of all things inspired of God. We thank God that you showed us God's orderly way so that we are now enjoying more intimate fellowship with Christ. The consciousness of the indwelling of the Holy Spirit has enriched our lives immensely.

Thank you for publishing your sermons. I am sure your book will continue to be a great help to us.

Again we wish to express our great appreciation for your loving services to us here. We shall be happy to remember you in our prayers and ask God to continue to bless your much needed ministry.

A grateful brother in Christ,"